# LIVING COURAGEOUSLY

# LIVING COURAGEOUSLY

By
RABBI SAMUEL CHIEL

KTAV PUBLISHING HOUSE, INC.
NEW YORK

COPYRIGHT © 1984
SAMUEL CHIEL

Library of Congress Cataloging in Publication Data

Chiel, Samuel.
   Living courageously.

   1. Jewish sermons—United States. 2. Sermons,
American—Jewish authors. I. Title.
BM740.2.C443   1984      296.4'2      84-7124
ISBN 0-88125-046-5

MANUFACTURED IN THE UNITED STATES OF AMERICA

To our wonderful children
Elizabeth and Hillel
David
Judy and Jonathan
and
To the loving memory of our
beloved brother,
Rabbi Arthur A. Chiel ז״ל

# TEMPLE EMANUEL PUBLICATION FUND DONORS

Charlotte and Irving Backman
Channah and Barouh Berkovits
Evelyn and Herbert Berman
Beth and Richard Blankstein
Joyce and Michael Bohnen
Eva Boorstein
Leslie and Robert Bornstein
Sally and Joseph Braunstein
Sonia Brezniak
Leon Brock
Barbara and Eliot Chertok
Lucille Cline
Marjorie and Gerald Drucker
Sybil and Alan M. Edelstein
Elaine and Gerald Elovitz
Ethel Epstein
Diane and David Feinzig
Esther and Sumner Feldberg
Linda and Michael Frieze
Anne Furman
Rae and Joseph Gann
Paula and Ralph Gilbert
Anita and David Granoff
Rosamond and Harvey Grant
Celia Greenbaum
Barbara and Steven Grossman
Ethel and Nissie Grossman
Jill and David Grossman
Shirley and Edgar Grossman

Sylvia and Morton Grossman
Shirley and Stanley Halperin
Evelyn and Harold Hindman
Dorothy and Clarence Jacobson
Dr. Trudy and Dr. Barry Karger
Beatrice and Mark Karofsky
Frances and Abraham Katz
Dr. Roselyn and Dr. Edwin Kolodny
Myra and Robert Kraft
Gertrude and Louis Lederman
Leona Levine
Madeline and Maurice Lifson
Miriam and Hyman Lockwood
Sonia and Joseph Michelson
Dorothy and George Miller
Nancy and Harold Parritz
Barbara and Dr. William Poplack
Miriam and Leonard Rosenblatt
Doris and Stanley Rosoff
Misha Rosoff
Hazel Santis
Ida and Harry Sher
Beatrice and David Sherter
Paula and Edwin Sidman
Edna and William Silverman
Louise and Alvin Slotnick
Marsha and Marc Slotnick
Edith and Herbert Sobol
Marcia and Robert Yanofsky

# Table of Contents

### GROWING HUMANLY
Preface ................................................. ix
1. Listening .............................................. 3
2. How to Manage Our Worries ............................ 7
3. A Second Chance....................................... 12
4. Our Feelings of Inadequacy............................ 16
5. How to Deal With Failure ............................. 19
6. Jealousy .............................................. 23
7. A Sustaining Vision................................... 27
8. Impossible Dreams .................................... 32
9. Where Are Our Treasures? ............................. 36
10. Why We Are Ungrateful................................ 40
11. Achieving Perspective ............................... 44
12. A Sense of Perspective .............................. 48
13. Be a *Mentch* ....................................... 52
14. How to Become a *Mentch* ............................ 56
15. Edward Steichen: A Mother's Influence ............... 60
16. Fathers and Sons .................................... 63
17. How to Judge People ................................. 68
18. How We Reveal Ourselves ............................. 72
19. Telling the Truth.................................... 77
20. When People Count ................................... 81
21. Requisites of the Good Life ......................... 86
22. The Letters of *Breshit*............................. 91
23. Why We Should Not Eat of the Tree of Knowledge ...... 95
24. Making a Will ....................................... 99
25. Taking an Incomplete ................................ 104
26. The Secret of a Long Life ........................... 107

### GROWING JEWISHLY
1. A Strategy for Jewish Renewal ........................ 113
2. What *Yom Kippur* Can Do for You...................... 118

3. Why We Survived ..................................... 121
4. The Art of Forgiveness ................................ 125
5. How to Celebrate a Jewish *Simcha* ..................... 129
6. Creating Great Jews .................................. 133
7. Three Unusual Bar Mitzvahs .......................... 137
8. Kindling the Spark .................................. 144
9. Hanukkah's Message Year Round ..................... 150
10. Falling in Love With Torah ........................... 154
11. The People of the Book ............................... 158
12. The Sabbath of Our Liberation ........................ 161
13. Entropy Versus Seder ................................ 164
14. The Importance of a Mitzvah ......................... 168
15. Total Involvement in a *Mitzvah* ...................... 171
16. Specialize in a *Mitzvah* .............................. 176
17. The Problem of Prayer ............................... 179
18. The Right Kind of Prayers ............................ 184
19. Private Prayer ....................................... 189

# Preface

Inertia is a great enemy. We become comfortable with our pattern of living even if occasionally we sense a momentary twinge of dissatisfaction and catch a fleeting glimpse of other possibilities for our lives.

Most of us lead busy lives and sometimes we are overwhelmed by our many commitments. We have little time or energy left for introspection and soul-searching.

And yet, Judaism insists that we must do better as people—in our relationships with others, in "educating" our emotions to become more accepting of people, in an appreciation of life and its many blessings.

The first section of this book, "Growing Humanly," is devoted to this purpose, to inspire us constantly to add to the sum total of our own *Mentchlichkeit*.

As Jews, most of us are too satisfied with our relationship with our Tradition. Some of us are very distant from Judaism and are not very troubled by our estrangement. This represents a pattern we established long ago.

Even if we are making progress in relating to our faith, a Jew must never be satisfied with what he or she has achieved. We need constantly to explore and renew our understanding of our Torah and its life-enhancing *mitzvot*, and we must deepen our responsibility for every Jew.

"Growing Jewishly" is the title and purpose of this book's second section. It is intended to spur us on to greater accomplishments in our quest for *Yiddishkeit*, so that each of us might become a positive and authentic Jew, ever more responsive to the beauty, truth, and goodness which is Judaism.

These sermons were preached over a period of five years to my beloved congregants and their friends at Temple Emanuel. Their generous response has been a source of great encouragement to me, and I hope that, in turn, these sermons have moved them to a greater love for their fellow Jews and fellow human beings.

I greatly appreciate the support of our dedicated President, Alan M. Edelstein, who has been a constant source of strength and encouragement to me.

I am most grateful to my dear friends, Evelyn and Herbert Berman, the Chairpersons of this project, together with the other donors whose generosity made this book possible.

I am indebted to my devoted secretary, Wilfredine Chiasson, who lovingly typed the manuscript and who has been a devoted friend to me and to our congregants.

Finally, to my beloved wife, Janet, for her love, encouragement, and willingness to share in the arduous life of the rabbinate, I am grateful each day.

1 ELUL 5743                                                August 10, 1983

# Growing Humanly

# 1.
# Listening

In several states there is a special course in counseling currently being offered to some unlikely people, to bartenders, beauticians, and cab drivers. It is a course in learning to listen better that will enable them to better counsel the many people who talk to them and tell them their troubles. As the director of one program in California explains, "The whole idea is to have people already hearing problems of the public, trained to more effectively handle them."

Why do so many people pour out their hearts to a bartender or a beautician? Because people are desperate for somebody, anybody, to listen to them. Have you ever had the experience of sitting next to a total stranger on a plane or train and finding that he or she is ready to tell you their life story and reveal some of their most intimate problems? There are simply not enough psychiatrists or psychologists available to listen to everybody who wants to ventilate his or her problems.

Recognizing the lack of enough therapists to listen to all the people who want to talk about their problems, two psychologists who are brothers, Charles and Warner Slack, have come up with a novel idea: why not have people tell their troubles to a computer? This is how it works: The person sits in front of a TV screen with an attached typewriter keyboard. The computer asks questions like, "Have you been feeling sad or down in the dumps?" "Do you have a problem with drugs?" "Do you have trouble expressing yourself?" If the person answers "Yes" to any of these questions, the computer then asks, for example, "You indicated earlier that you had been feeling sad or down in the dumps" (or whatever problem had been indicated). Would you like to talk about this?"

In an experiment with thirty-two volunteers from colleges in the Boston area, the psychologists found that, though the large majority of the students preferred speaking to live therapists, almost all of them were willing to discuss intimate problems with the computer and said that they felt better afterward. People are desperate to have somebody to speak to, even to a computer, if necessary.

Why are people so desperate for somebody to listen? Many lonely people have nobody to talk to. But even those who are not lonely, like couples who are married, parents with children, people who have friends and associates at work, even they are equally desperate because people don't really listen to each other.

People may hear us but they don't really listen to what we are saying. There are a number of reasons why they don't listen. Some people are simply not interested. For example, a political candidate may be greeting people. He clasps everybody's hands and says "Wonderful" to everything. If you go through that line and say to him, "My grandmother was killed an hour ago," he will probably respond with "Wonderful" and turn to the next person. He is not really interested in you as a person. He is really seeking your vote and, therefore, he wants to "press your flesh" not listen to your problems.

Sometimes people don't listen to each other because they are preoccupied with their own problems. A husband may not be able to listen to his wife if he is worried about his business. His wife may not be able to concentrate on his problems for the same reason, because of her preoccupation with her work or with her children.

Sometimes people will stop telling us their problems because we are so judgmental. A friend begins to tell you something about which he feels guilty, but when he sees your shock or your disapproving frown he will likely stop talking, knowing that you do not have a receptive ear.

Sometimes we don't listen because we overreact. A child may confide in us that he skipped school one day. Instead of viewing this as a temporary aberration, we see before us the vision of a child who will likely turn into a "bum." Our reaction may be so extreme that our child will hesitate to confide in us in the future.

People are desperate for somebody to listen to them but most of us don't know how to listen. Listening well is a great art and it needs to be cultivated. How should we listen to each other? When I was a student at the Seminary, I took a course in pastoral counseling at Bellevue Hospital. Our instructor told us, "In whatever problem you are dealing with, you may harm a person by saying the wrong thing, but you can never do any harm by listening." Each of us needs to recognize that simply by listening, even if we don't have a solution for the person's problem, that act is in itself therapeutic and can be of great help to another person.

We also have to learn to listen to another with understanding, with what the renowned psychoanalyst Theodore Reik called, "Listening With the Third Ear." You have to ask yourself, "What is this person really saying? What is he really trying to tell me?"

A man came to a Hasidic Rabbi before Passover and asked him if he could give him enough money to buy wine for *Yom Tov*. The Rabbi gave him a large sum, far more than was required for the purchase of wine. When the Rabbi's wife asked him why he had given the man so much more than he had requested, he explained, "What this man was embarrassed to say was that he had no money to provide food for his family on Passover. That's why I gave him enough for all his Passover needs."

In addition, we have to listen with empathy, which means to avoid being judgmental or critical. We always need to remember the great teaching of Hillel: *Al tadin et chavercha ad shetagia limkomo.* "Do not judge another person until you stand in his place." If somebody is telling you about a sin or error he or she has committed or about something his child has done about which he is greatly embarrassed, do not take it upon yourself to judge that person or the child. Instead, listen with empathy and say to yourself, "There but for the grace of God go I and my child." You may simply have had a little more *mazel* than he.

Finally, we have to learn to listen with total attentiveness. I think that perhaps the most moving story I have ever heard is the one told by the great Jewish philosopher and mystic, Martin Buber. One day, he was engrossed in a mood of mystical ecstasy when a young man came to see him. Buber spoke with him pleasantly and was polite to him and the young man left. Subsequently, Buber learned that this man was about to be drafted into the army and he wanted to consult with Buber on questions of life and death. Soon thereafter the young man committed suicide. Buber felt that he was responsible, for he had not listened to him as attentively as he should have. Buber never forgave himself and subsequently he developed the philosophy which he called "I-Thou," in which he insisted that we must never look upon another person as an "it," as an object for our use and exploitation, but that each person must be seen and related to as a "Thou," a unique, precious, and irreplaceable human being created in the image of God.

Buber, therefore, summed up his understanding of religion with these words: "For me this is what I mean by religion—not removing yourself into another world, but responding to the call that comes into your everyday life. Above all, listening to both the silent and the spoken voices when one person speaks to another, so that together they can remove the barrier between two human beings."

If we train ourselves to really listen to others, we will have less need to speak to bartenders, beauticians, and cabbies, maybe even to psychologists and psychiatrists. If we listen well, we will begin to hear and respond to each other's silent cry for comfort, strength, and love.

# 2.
# How to Manage Our Worries

Everybody has worries. Some people worry about their health, some about their business. When we are younger, we worry about our grades in school and about getting into college. Some worries are legitimate and even helpful.

If a man loses his job and he has to support his family, he has a legitimate worry about the future, and perhaps the worry can help him find another job.

If you are walking on a street at night in any of the cities of our country today, there is a legitimate reason to be worried. Perhaps that worry might even be helpful to you because you are more alert to the possible dangers.

But I would submit to you that most of us worry about matters over which we have no control, and the effects of these worries are baneful and harmful to us.

A great many of us worry over the past. When we have problems with our children, for example, we ask ourselves over and over, "Where did I fail? Why didn't I do better?" We agonize, we weep, we worry over the past, and we blame ourselves for every misfortune.

There is another kind of worry that so many of us are plagued with; we worry about the future. We wonder: Will I be successful in my job? Will my son marry the right kind of girl? When we are younger, we worry about whether we will be popular at school, whether we will be able to make friends. Sometimes we conjure up in our minds every conceivable disaster, to the point that we are sometimes afraid to face another day.

Just as there are specialists in every field, there are also specialists in the art of worrying. There are some people who have a worry for every occasion. A psychologist recently wrote about one of his patients who came to see him because of his tremendous anxiety. He was economically insecure and constantly lived in dread of losing his job. During the course of the treatment, the patient was informed that he had received a large bequest from an uncle who had died. For several weeks the man was elated, but he soon returned to the psychologist, terribly worried about his investments.

I know a lady who is a "worry specialist," who tells me that she gets very worried if she finds that she has nothing to worry about.

Ralph Waldo Emerson once wrote:

> Some of your hurts you have cured
> And the sharpest you have survived,
> But what torments of grief you endured
> From evils that never arrived.

What are the effects of this kind of worry that besets so many of us? The whole field of psychosomatic medicine deals with the many physical ailments from which people suffer as a result of the anxieties that beset them. Physicians believe that ulcers, heart disease, blood pressure, asthma and other allergies often stem from the fact that we are bedeviled by anxieties. Most of us find, when we are really worried, that we cannot sleep well, we lose interest in what we are doing, and we sometimes become paralyzed and ineffectual.

Long ago there was a wise Jewish teacher in the Book of Proverbs who recognized the debilitating effects of worry when he taught:

> *De'agah b'lev ish yashchenah:*
> "Anxiety in a person's heart weighs him down."

The question I would like to consider with you is this: is there any way to control our worries? If we cannot eliminate them altogether, can we at least make them more manageable? Permit me to make several suggestions.

The Talmud records an incisive comment by a Rabbi in reference to the verse that I just cited from the Book of Proverbs. He suggests that if you will make a slight change in the vocalization of the last word, you will find the beginning of a solution. According to his suggestion, the verse should be read:

> *De'agah b'lev ish yesichenah:*
> "If there is anxiety in a person's heart, let him talk about it."

How important it is to be able to have a good friend to whom you are able to talk about your own worries and concerns. In Yiddish we use the expression *Optzureden zich fun hartz*. To be able to speak to somebody about the worries that trouble us most is the beginning of the solution. To be able to talk to a husband or a wife who is understanding enough to listen to our worries, to be able to speak to somebody who is not so preoccupied with his own concerns that he can listen to what we are really saying, is of major help in learning to manage our worries.

To be the kind of parents to whom a child can come with a problem, to talk to us about his worries at any time in his life, is to be the kind of parents who are a never-ending blessing to their children.

At times, if our anxiety becomes overwhelming and we cannot function in our work or in our relationships, we ought not to be embarrassed to seek professional help, to go to a person who is professionally trained to listen, to understand, and to help us with our problems. Such a person can be of tremendous help in our time of greatest need. I would suggest, therefore, that the first element in learning to manage our own worries and anxieties is to talk to somebody whom we can trust about those worries that trouble us most.

A second aspect to the art of managing our worries is never to permit ourselves to become so totally preoccupied with ourselves or with our families that we simply have no room left for the rest of the world. My guess is that if you would confine any person to his own home for too long a period in a state of inactivity, he will find an infinite variety of things to worry about.

What we must do is to keep our minds perpetually active. In most areas, for example, there are so many magnificent offerings in Adult Education and in university courses. There is no excuse for us to sit at home and agonize over all kinds of worries. Instead, we should take all kinds of courses in order to partake of the great wisdom that civilization has created. We have great books in the Jewish tradition and in the tradition of mankind that ought not to be left in the libraries or even on our own shelves at home. We ought to read them to keep our minds active through the pleasure and stimulation they will bring us.

Not only should we keep our minds active. We should also involve ourselves with great causes that are far more lasting in their influence than our own individual lives. Look at the great causes that beckon to us today: a cause like Israel that needs help from every one of us. Or take the cause of Russian Jews, who are crying, praying, and hoping that somebody, somewhere, will raise his voice to demand that they be freed from their Soviet bondage. There are people who need help in every community, patients in hospitals, residents of homes for the aged, children who need help in learning to read, in learning how to cope with society. We have the mind, the strength, and the ability to be of help to countless numbers of people. When a person makes his purview not only himself and his own family but goes outside the confines of his own home, looks around, and finds the thousands of vital causes that are beckoning to him for help, he will never permit himself to become obsessed with himself and his own worries.

Finally, I would like to suggest a third element to the art of managing our worries. Let me refer again to those people who worry about the past and the future. For those who worry about the past, may I suggest this rule: don't worry about those things you cannot change. To say to yourself over and over again, "Why did I fail?" will not help the problem. Very likely you are blaming yourself for a situation that has a multiplicity of reasons of which you may be only one and perhaps not even the most important factor.

Instead of becoming paralyzed by guilt and worry, ask yourself the question: "Can I learn from the past, from my mistakes and my experience, so that I can do better now?" That is the question that really counts.

Remember how a little child learns to walk? He falls, picks himself up, falls again, and then gets up again. Slowly and laboriously, he begins to walk with steadiness and ease. Each one of us has to learn about life the same way. We fall down, we fail, sometimes we do not do as well as we would like, but it is possible to pick ourselves up, to begin to walk again, and to achieve many significant accomplishments.

For those people who worry about the future, I would suggest another rule: don't worry about those things that may never happen. The Talmud puts it very succinctly by saying:

*Dayah l'tzarah b'shaatah:*
"Take one problem at a time and deal with the problem that is before you now."

Don't worry about the infinitude of possible problems that might develop in the future.

A colleague received a letter recently from a very wise man, now in his eighties, who deals with the problem of worry out of the richness of his own wisdom and experience. This is what he wrote:

> One thing I have learned from life—it took time to teach it to me, and I feel it will help others if you care to pass it on. Wait till you are fifty years of age (one does not have much sense before that time of life), and you will find that the things you worry most about seldom happen in the way you feared. Or if they do happen, and sometimes they do, they turn out differently from what you anticipated. It may seem a strange thing to say but the real troubles of life are almost never the things you worry about. As often as not, they are things we have not dreamed of. The wise thing to do is to form the habit of waiting before worrying, and you will find that the thing you might have worried over never turns up, and if it does, it is modified by other things.

I think there is a great deal of wisdom in that letter, especially in the phrase "waiting before worrying." The capacity to wait without anxiety and to endure with confidence is what is sometimes called faith. Such faith issues from the most profound wisdom of the human experience.

Let us not agonize over the past which is gone, and let us not worry over a future which may never happen. Instead, let us fill our lives with *mitzvot*, which will bring us closer to God and to His children. For a life preoccupied with *mitzvot* has little room left for the worries that can destroy our souls.

# 3.
# A Second Chance

What would happen if you found that you could not celebrate Passover because you were far away from your family and your home, and you could not find any *matzot* or wine or any of the other necessities for *Yom Tov* where you happened to be? I am sure that you would feel terrible, having been deprived of one of the most precious moments of the Jewish year when Jews love to be together with their families, to celebrate together our great Festival of Freedom.

There is a very similar situation described in our Torah reading. At the time of Passover, several men were in a state of ritual impurity and they were therefore unable to offer the Passover sacrifice on the fourteenth day of Nisan, the day prescribed by the Torah. They came to Moses in great agitation and said to him: "Why should we be deprived of the opportunity of celebrating Passover?"

In response, Moses said that he would commune with God to learn the answer from Him. The Torah then relates that God taught Moses a new law which said that if a person is impure or at a great distance from the Sanctuary, making it impossible for him to celebrate Passover on the prescribed date, he should celebrate the festival one month later, on the fourteenth day of the Hebrew month Iyar. This Holy Day was to be called *Pesach Shaynee*, the Second Passover, so that each person would be able to celebrate *Pesach* together with his own family, even if it was delayed.

This incident is a striking example of the flexibility of Jewish law. Where there is need for a change, God Himself insists that it be made. But in addition, this passage reflects a beautiful insight into the way that God deals with human beings.

*Pesach Shaynee*, a second Passover, implies that God always gives us another chance. Not only does He enable us to celebrate Passover a second time but, as a matter of fact, this Divine concession is the central theme of the most important Holy Days of the Jewish year,

*Rosh Hashanah* and *Yom Kippur*. *Teshuvah*, penitence, means that there is a possibility for human beings to change and improve their lives, regardless of how far they have strayed. What those days say to us and what *teshuvah* teaches us is that God is always willing to take us back, accept us, to give us another chance in life.

Very often, however, we refuse to do the same for God's children. There are people in our society whom we try to discard and to whom we often refuse to give another chance at life.

Take, for example, those people who serve time in prison. Once a man has a record, we are reluctant to give him a job. We are unwilling to accept him into society. We make an implicit assumption: once a man has been convicted of a crime, he will inevitably commit another crime!

Former prisoners are not the only people to whom we are not willing to give a second chance. We are also uncomfortable with people who have recovered from mental illness. We pity them but we avert our eyes from them. We assume that once having been mentally ill, they will never be quite the same again.

But we often go even further than that. We even refuse to give a second chance to people who are very close to us. Sometimes there are people who have a good friend with whom they have had a quarrel, and they refuse to speak to their friend ever again. Sometimes there are husbands and wives who permit their differences to grow into a state of chronic anger, whose words become weapons to be used against each other in a cruel, unending war. Sometimes there are parents and children who hurt each other so much that they stop communicating with each other altogether. They live in the same home but they are like ships passing in the night. All too often we refuse to give another chance even to those who are closest to us.

Why do you think God gives each of us a second chance? Because He has had a great deal of experience with us, and it has not always been the best kind of experience. He knows how frail we are, and He affirms the words of the prophet Jeremiah:

*Akov halev mikol v'anush hu mi yadaenu:*
The heart is deceitful above all things, and it is exceedingly weak, who can understand it?

We ourselves often cannot understand our own motivations. Therefore, the Rabbis say, when God judges His children, He leaves

His *Kisay Hadin*, the Throne of Justice, and is seated instead on the *Kisay Harachamim*, His Throne of Mercy. For if God were to judge us by the strict standards of justice, who would ever emerge before Him blameless and pure? God always gives us a second chance because He knows all too well our foibles and our weaknesses.

In fairness, should we not do the same in judging those people in human society who suffer most? When we judge those who have been in prison, should we not ask ourselves the question: if we faced the same temptations, if we grew up with the same deprivation, if we were confronted with the same provocations, would we have stood the test or might we be in their situation?

When we consider those who suffer from mental illness, should we not ask ourselves the question: if we had been subject to the same pressures, if we had suffered the same traumas, if we had been struck by the same blows of fate, might we not be in their place? Mental illness, after all, can afflict any one of us with the same impartiality as physical illness.

And if we are angry with a good friend, is it not possible that we have also offended our friends? And if we are angry with our spouse, do we not both share in the culpability? Have we then been completely perfect in our relationship with the person we love?

And if communication has ceased between us and our children, should we then not ask ourselves: have we been as understanding and as encouraging as we should have been or have we also contributed to the hostility that embitters our homes and our lives?

The reason God gives us another chance is because he understands our weaknesses, and for the same reason, we ought to do the same for one another.

What happens to us when God gives us another chance? It is, in effect, as if God were saying to each one of us: there is no situation in life that is altogether hopeless. Even if I did not observe the first Passover, I can still observe the second Passover. Even if I have wandered very far from my faith and my principles, the concept of *teshuvah* says that life is never hopeless; that it is possible for me to try again to become a *Mentch*; and that if my effort is sincere, God will welcome me back once again.

The same thing happens to society's rejected people when we give them another chance. A man who has a record and yet finds that there are people who are willing to give him a job learns that it is possible to go straight; that there are some people who do believe in him; that there are some people who are willing to lend a helping hand; and that there are some people who do not subscribe to the primitive and cruel notion that a criminal must be punished forever.

A person who has had a mental illness, if we are accepting of him, can find that he can be more productive than before; that he can function in his job again; that people understand that mental illness is not a cause for embarrassment but recognize that it can happen to anybody, even to the strongest of us. If we give the rejected human beings of society another chance, they, too, can begin to feel that life is not hopeless.

When we relate to those with whom we are closest, if we are willing to give them another chance, we will also see that the gaps that divide us need not be permanent.

If I am angry with a friend, my anger need not be permanent. A telephone call, a visit, or handshake can sometimes bridge the gap, even today.

If there is hostility between my spouse and myself, it need not remain between us forever. An understanding word, a smile, a kiss, can assuage a world of anger, even today.

And if we are locked in combat with our children, it need not be our permanent destiny. A discussion, an honest expression of our real feelings and a willingness to listen to the other person's feelings, a genuine acceptance of the other person's individuality, can begin a whole new chapter in our relationships with each other, even today.

Do you remember the stirring biblical account of Israel standing at Mount Sinai listening to the revelation of God? But soon thereafter, Moses leaves the people to go up to the mountain, tarries a bit, and the people begin to worship the Golden Calf. Do you remember Moses descending the mountain and smashing the *Luchot Habrit*, the Tablets of the Covenant, in his anger with the people who had so recently heard from God and who now already deny His existence?

But then the Torah tells us that when Israel repented, Moses brought from the mountain a second set of the Tablets of the Law, and it was *these* Tablets that guided, encouraged, and accompanied our people through their wandering in the wilderness and their settling in the land of Canaan. The first Tablets were destroyed but our future as a people was not doomed because God was willing to give us another chance. And it was the second Tablets of the Covenant, not the first, that kept us alive as a people and that enabled us to reach this day.

God always gives us a second chance. It is left to us to do the same for His children.

# 4.
# Our Feelings of Inadequacy

In today's Torah reading we read of the ill-fated reconnaissance mission sent by Moses to Canaan. The result was a disaster. Ten men, leaders of the people, returned with this report: "We will not be able to overcome this people; they are too strong for us." The people of Canaan, they reported, were "giants"—

> *Vanehi V'Eyneynu Kachagavim:*
> "We were in our own sight like grasshoppers."

When the Israelites heard this report, they panicked and wanted to return to Egypt. Therefore, God ultimately recognized that these former slaves were not capable of acquiring the Promised Land. Only their children would be able to do so, those who had already been born free.

Why did the majority of this mission return with such a pessimistic report? Their words were very revealing, especially about their feelings about themselves:

> *Vanehi V'Eyneynu Kachagavim:*
> "We were in our own eyes like grasshoppers."

They felt inadequate to the great challenge before them; they gave up before they even *saw* the land; they were helpless from the very beginning of their mission.

They are not the only people to feel inadequate. I think they suffered from a malady which many of us share. We walk around with a gnawing sense of our own inadequacy, our own unworthiness, our own feelings of helplessness in the face of life's constant buffeting.

For instance, there are students who feel they are not doing well enough in school; if they do poorly on an exam, they are shattered emotionally.

When a patient dies, the physician feels depressed; he feels that he has failed. When a writer's book is criticized by a reviewer, the writer may feel that he is a worthless hack. A rabbi finds himself often wondering: is anybody listening?

We have feelings of inadequacy about our relationships as well. Parents wonder why their children are so angry with them, why they seem to delight in doing the opposite of what they suggest to them.

Why do we feel this way? Why do we feel so inadequate so much of the time?

For some, it is a result of our childhood self-image. Our parents might have said to us:

"You are so lazy, you will never accomplish anything in life."

"Look at your brother—why can't you be like him?"

Or a teacher may have said to us:

"Why do you have to do everything wrong!"

"Why can't you be like the boy next to you?"

"Why can't you figure that out—it's so simple!"

Our friends may have helped, too. When we played baseball and the teams were chosen, you were chosen last. Maybe you weren't as quick as the others and the kids made fun of you and laughed.

Most of us are still walking around with feelings of inadequacy, some of which have come from our past, voices within us that never seem to disappear.

There is another reason for our feelings of inadequacy. We have a tendency to take one failure and generalize from it to our entire life.

When a patient dies, the physician says, "I have failed completely."

When a book is panned, the writer says, "I have lost my talent."

When some people do not respond, the Rabbi says, "Nobody is listening."

When a child does not fulfill our dreams, we say, "I have failed as a parent."

Is there a solution to this problem of inadequacy? We may not be able to undo our own past but we can learn how to deal with children better. When a child spills milk all over the table, we should not say, "You are so clumsy. You always drop things!" Instead, we should simply say, "Here is a towel. Please wipe it up."

The teacher should not say, "You are a terrible student," but instead, "I know you can do better." And when the student does better, the teacher should not say, "I didn't think you had it in you," but rather, "I knew you could do it. That's great!"

But there is something we can do about our own inadequacy. We must learn not to generalize from one failure nor permit it to become a judgment upon our whole lives. No life is full of success. Each person has his own failures, sometimes in his work, sometimes with those he loves, sometimes in a dream that is never realized. Only to the outsider does it appear that some people get all the breaks, that some families have only successes, that some people have cornered the market on happiness.

There is a Yiddish proverb which says:

*Dacht Zich Az Bai Yenem Lacht Zich:*
"It always appears as if the other person is really happy."

Each of us fails and yet each of us is a far greater success than we realize. The physician saves so many lives in his practice. The writer gives inspiration and pleasure to so many readers. The Rabbi inspires some people to become better Jews and better people. And as parents, with all our failures, what we do has an impact; our children usually turn out far better than we had expected.

In the Midrash we are told that God was very annoyed with the spies because they saw themselves as grasshoppers and, as a result, the Canaanites also looked upon them in the same way. Whereupon He reproached them for their negative attitude, saying:

*Mi Yomahr Shelo Heyitem B'Eyneyhem K'Mahlachim:*
"How do you know? Perhaps in their eyes you appeared as angels."

Perhaps the best cure for our feelings of inadequacy is to know that there are so many to whom we do not appear as grasshoppers but as angels. If only we knew how much we mean to others, whether we are doctors, writers, rabbis, teachers or students, parents or children, husbands or wives, perhaps we would belittle ourselves far less.

Each one of us means far more than we can ever know to so many who depend on us, need us, and love us; without us, their lives would be diminished and empty; with us, their lives have hope, beauty, and meaning.

# 5.
# How to Deal With Failure

Our society places a great premium on success. Every parent wants his or her child to be successful. The most popular books on the bestseller list are usually entitled: *How to Be Successful in Business, How to Be a Successful Investor, How to Be a Successful Lover.* Because we are so preoccupied with success, we avoid thinking about failure.

Failure may lurk in the background as an ominous possibility, but somehow we hope that if we don't talk about it, we can prevent it from happening to us. Because we refuse to talk about it and face it openly, our fear of failure may overwhelm us and, at times, even destroy us. Do you remember Bobby Fischer? He was the remarkable genius who, until a few years ago, reigned as the chess champion of the world. In 1975 he was supposed to defend his title against Anatoly Karpov. Chess experts knew that Karpov didn't stand a chance against Fischer. But Fischer refused to play. Some people thought it was because of his desire for publicity and that he would show up for the match at the last minute; he simply wanted the world to focus on his delaying tactics. But amazingly, he never did show up, and on April 3, 1975, the President of the World Chess Organization declared Anatoly Karpov to be the new world champion. For the first time in history a man became the chess champion of the world without proving his right to the crown in a showdown match.

Why did Bobby Fischer refuse to play? He had demanded that the match, which would be won in ten victories, should be declared a tie if the score reached nine victories for each player. When the World Chess Organization refused to accede to his demand, Fischer's irrational fear of defeat during that final game compelled him to relinquish his title rather than play. His fear was irrational because Karpov didn't even approximate Fischer's ability. Yet Fischer refused to play because for him defeat would have meant the destruction of his ego, and this fear ultimately destroyed him as a champion. By losing the championship, he not only lost the prestige of that position but at the same time he also lost a fee of five million dollars. Somehow, Bobby Fischer never learned that each of us, even the most successful, may at times suffer defeat. He never learned that even if we fail at one time or another, we need not necessarily consider ourselves failures. He never learned that the fear of failure may even be worse than failure itself.

Those who have had the experience of failing and who are not afraid to talk about their defeats tell us that failing is not all bad. It is even possible to learn from failure some very important lessons.

Jules Pfeiffer, the brilliant cartoonist and playwright, has often experienced failure in his life. As a matter of fact, he says flatly, "I've done more failing than succeeding." When he was young, he reveals, "I thought of myself as a total flop as a child. I was docile, passive, unaggressive, non-athletic. I thought I'd make it as an adult if I could just get past gym!"

He had problems with his mother:

> My mother had a passion for cleaning house. I had two sisters and we were always cleaning house. And she was always finding fault with the way we cleaned. Then there were lectures on the outside world, how everyone was out to get us.
>
> Someone you love shouldn't be deceiving you. She was giving me advice counter to my instincts. It was an awful discovery. Her judgments were wrong. I couldn't trust the judgments of someone I love. I felt isolated. Then I was left to my own device, my own discoveries.

Pfeiffer says that each person has to take risks, even if it means failing at times. "When I started out, well-meaning adults gave me well-meaning advice that resulted in one failure after another. When I ignored the well-meaning, I had one success after another. Well-meaning advice is often safe and therefore riskless. It should be ignored."

If you are not careful, he warns, failure can do terrible things to you. "You can fail and failure can make you bitter. I have seen extremely talented people of extraordinary wit turn sour and nasty. They always seem to hurt only themselves. I took this as an object lesson. I always told myself: 'No matter what, I must not be bitter.' I reminded myself that it was my decision to become a cartoonist and that a cartoonist can fail easily. When I have failed, I told myself that I couldn't be mad—except in a temporary way. So I got over it. Failure is like a bad cold. You recover."

Finally, he sums up his experience with failure with these words: "Life functions like a draft. A draft is raw material that becomes refined and more refined. The refinements are the weeding out of the mistakes. You cannot realize where you went wrong until you've made mistakes. Your mistakes teach you what not to do the next time."

If we use the experience of our failures well, Pfeiffer reminds us, and if we do not permit ourselves to become bitter, we can learn how to do better the next time. From a divorce, it is possible to learn how to create a better marriage the next time. When we hurt someone we love, we can learn to be more sensitive next time. When we become enraged over some inconsequential pettiness, we can determine to take a larger perspective in the future.

Someone once put it this way: "The only complete catastrophe is the catastrophe from which we learn nothing."

Perhaps the most important lesson each of us needs in life is to learn how to face failure when it happens to us. We can brood about it and nurse our bruises for the rest of our lives. Or we can accept its pain and not let it defeat us. Ellen Goodman, the popular *Globe* columnist, had a father who ran for Congress when she was a teenager. She and the other members of her family licked stamps, took the day off to work at the polls, stayed up late to listen to the returns, heard the issues and strategies discussed in the living room. She saw people come up to her father in adulation and she also heard a man, while throwing the campaign literature back at her, shout, "I wouldn't vote for him if he was the last man on earth."

Her father lost the race and this is how she describes his reaction: "The next morning, defeated and deeply in debt, my father put on his suit and his tie and his optimism and went to the office. It was this last gesture that was imprinted on my psyche more than perhaps any other. I learned from my father, the candidate, that this is what a grown-up does. When life disappoints you, when the world takes a whack at you, you still get up, get dressed and go back to work." Ellen Goodman says that she learned more from her father by observing him than from his words. He died at age fifty-seven of a malignancy which prevented this articulate man from speaking. But she writes that whenever she experiences difficulties and setbacks in her own life, she always hears these words saying to her, "Get up, get dressed, go back to work."

Her father taught Ellen Goodman a lesson about failing that we all need to learn. We cannot know what defeats and difficulties life may hold in store for us but we can determine to face them unflinchingly and without fear and continue to do what we must, for our work, our families, and ourselves, so that life will never defeat us.

A great poet once wrote this prayer which each of us needs to learn: "Let me not pray to be sheltered from dangers but to be fearless in facing them. Let me not beg for the stilling of my pain but for the heart to conquer it. Let me not look for allies in life's battlefield, but to my own strength. Let me not crave in anxious fear to be saved, but hope for the patience to win my freedom. Grant me that I may not be a coward, feeling your mercy in my success alone; but let me find the grasp of your hand in my failure."

# 6.
# Jealousy

Joseph Kennedy, father of the late President John Kennedy, once said, "More men die of jealousy than cancer."

This is precisely the meaning of today's Torah reading. *Korach*, of the tribe of Levi, is a member of the same tribe as Moses and Aaron and he is consumed by jealousy of these two men who, according to the Midrash, are his first cousins. Moses is the leader of Israel and Aaron is the High Priest. What about Korach; why wasn't he given any of these high honors? In anger, he shouts at them, *"Rav lachem"*—You have taken too much power for yourselves. *"Umadua titnasoo al k'hal adonai"*—Why do you raise yourselves above the rest of us? In his jealousy, Korach precipitates a major crisis for Moses and Aaron. He foments a major rebellion against their authority until, ultimately, he and his followers are destroyed.

We all share that feeling of Korach's jealousy. We envy those who are wealthier than us. We resent those who have more power than us. When our colleagues are honored, we begrudge them their recognition. Even when we watch other people's children receiving awards, we find ourselves feeling upset and unhappy.

Are you familiar with the *ayin hara*, the evil eye? I am sure that you have heard the expression *Kein ayin hora*, a phrase used to guard against the depredations of the *ayin hara*. We think of the *ayin hara* as a superstition and we are right. This is the reason why a parent and child are not supposed to follow each other for an *aliyah*. It seems silly, doesn't it? I was startled to read a traditional commentator recently who gives quite a different interpretation to *ayin hara*. He says it is not a mysterious evil spirit. It is people who are watching, and when they see something good happening to you, they begrudge you your happiness. That's the *ayin hara* you really have to worry about.

More people die of jealousy than cancer.

Why are people so jealous of each other? Perhaps it all starts in the family, in the sibling rivalry that develops between sisters and brothers. As children, we are jealous of each other, thinking at times that our brother or sister is our parents' favorite child and is being treated better than us. In the family, we usually vie with each other for our parents' attention, recognition, and love.

Can you imagine what would happen if a parent would give one child a larger portion of ice cream than the other? The result would likely be mayhem. The ice cream takes on a larger meaning than just being delicious food. It is a symbol of the parents' love, and if my brother or sister gets more than I do, it's obvious that my parents love them more than me.

I remember an incident at camp one summer. The kitchen staff had somehow miscalculated and one division didn't get ice cream. We almost had a riot on our hands. The campers protested: why did the rest of the camp get ice cream but not they? We finally mollified them by promising to give them, and only them, larger portions of ice cream the following day.

We carry over those same feelings of rivalry into adulthood. When somebody else has wealth, power, or honor, we ask ourselves: why does he or she deserve it more than I? When somebody else's child receives an award, we ask ourselves: why should such good things happen to their child and not to mine? Like the ice cream when we were children, we are angry if good things happen to others instead of to us, and we resent the fact that others seem to be getting more attention, recognition, and love than we.

Somehow, when we see something good happening to another we feel it to be a diminishing of ourselves. Somehow we become less worthy because of their accomplishments. The writer Gore Vidal expresses what most of us would never admit when he says, "Every time a friend succeeds, I die a little."

Is there a solution to this problem of jealousy which besets us all? There are several measures I would like to suggest to you. First, like Joseph Kennedy, each of us needs to realize that jealously is a terrible disease. The Surgeon General ought to label it like cigarettes: "Jealousy may be dangerous to your health." One of the rabbis of the Talmud put it very strongly: *Hakinah v'hataavah v'hakavod motzeein et haadam min haolam*. "Envy, desire and the quest for honor drive a person out of the world." What he meant was that each of those qualities can destroy a person's relationships with other human beings and can make life miserable and wretched. Envy of others can make us into seething, resentful, angry people, at war with the world. Envy can turn us into "grievance collectors." It can make us believe that we always get the short end of the stick, that our lane on the road is always the slowest to move, that our seat in the theater is always the worst in the house. To find a cure for the condition, we need first to accept the fact that jealousy is a dangerous, corrosive disease—doing us a great deal of harm.

Second, we need to remind ourselves regularly that each of us, in our own way, accomplishes important things, even though we may not receive as much recognition as others.

If I do my work honestly and effectively, work of which I can be proud, that is an important accomplishment.

If I give of myself and do volunteer work for an important cause, that is an indispensable accomplishment.

If I am an understanding son or daughter to parents who are growing older and who are becoming dependent upon me, that is a significant accomplishment.

If I am a good husband or wife and help to create a lasting and fulfilling relationship with another, that is a major accomplishment.

If I am a good parent and help to raise a child who will have the potential of making something of his or her life, that is a great accomplishment.

In my former congregation there was a man who used to invite an old friend, who was very wealthy, to share his Seder with him. The host would lead the Seder, with its songs, discussion, and fun, surrounded by his children and grandchildren. Once, after the Seder, when the rest of the family had dispersed, the wealthy man, with tears in his eyes, quietly said to his host, "My children and I have been estranged for many years. I would give everything I own to have one Seder like yours with my own family."

To fight our feelings of envy, each of us needs to remind ourself of our own accomplishments and to realize that others' accomplishments in no way diminish our own.

The final and most difficult step in the cure of jealousy is to train ourselves to accept others' achievements by a specific action. This will be very difficult at first, but we have to begin by congratulating people for something good that they have accomplished, even if it hurts us to do it, and even if we don't really mean it.

As we train ourselves to do this regularly and as we see the kind of joy we bring to others, we may even begin to mean what we say. And slowly, imperceptibly, we may even begin to enjoy the other person's achievement. When that happens, we will discover that our own life can become far more enjoyable and fulfilling. Instead of celebrating the rare, occasional *simcha* we have in our own life, we will now be able to fill our life with the *simchas* and joys of many others.

We will thereby make ourselves into the kind of people able to share other people's happiness and also their pain and sorrow; we will be able to identify with other human beings; we will, in short, transform ourselves from people who are consumed and destroyed by envy to those who continually grow in the direction of greater acceptance, concern, and empathy for every human being.

# 7.
# A Sustaining Vision

What are our feelings when we leave home for the first time for a vacation? There is a feeling of anticipation of a new experience. But at the same time there is a fear of leaving the familiar for the unfamiliar. We wonder what it will be like when we reach our destination. We also experience a sense of loneliness. We miss our parents, our brothers and sisters, even though we occasionally fight with them.

Imagine then the feelings of Jacob as he left home for the first time but not for a vacation! He was leaving because he had conspired with his mother, Rebekkah, to steal the firstborn blessing from Esau, and Esau wanted to kill him.

Jacob had always lived a very sheltered life, meditative, contemplative, his mother's favorite, apparently a good cook. Imagine this sheltered person running away from home, to an uncle whom he didn't know, who lived very far away, and could only be reached by traveling through the arduous perils of the desert.

The Torah does not tell us about Jacob's feelings. It is up to us to intuit them from what we know of him and the circumstances in which he found himself. I have the feeling that Jacob must have been in a state of despair.

Despair, first, because of his intense loneliness. Away from his home for the first time, away from his mother who constantly worried about him and hovered over him, wrenched away from everything familiar, all alone in a vast and terrifying desert. When he finally fell asleep, he had to use a stone as a pillow.

The truth is that in each life there are moments of great loneliness when we feel utterly desolate and alone.

As parents, when our last child goes away to school, the house becomes so big and so empty. When a husband or wife dies, the other person is filled with grief. Everything familiar becomes so painful: the chair he sat on; the books she loved; reading the different sections of the newspaper and making comments to each other.

Elderly parents whose children live out of town often suffer this loneliness. I know one woman who says to me whenever I see her, "I am alone like a stone."

Like Jacob, we all have our moments of terrifying loneliness.

But Jacob left home with a special burden. He had grown up with his good-natured, easygoing brother, and though their interests were very different, they liked each other. Now, suddenly, because of Jacob's deception, Esau was bewildered and furious and in his rage wanted to strike out and kill him. Jacob must have been overwhelmed by feelings of guilt and remorse over what he had done to his trusting brother, adding even more intensity to his feelings of despair.

We, too, have our struggles with feelings of guilt like Jacob. We feel guilty when we know we have cheated somebody, even if we rationalize our action. We feel guilty when we hurt another person, even though we try to justify our action. We feel guilty when we are impatient with someone we love, even though we have a ready explanation for our response.

And there is something particularly terrible about a feeling of guilt. It can stay on and plague us for many years, long after the incident is over.

Do you remember the remarkable confrontation between Joseph and his brothers in Egypt? Joseph was the Prime Minister and the brothers had come to beg him for food. They did not recognize this royal personage but he recognized them. He called them spies and demanded that they bring their younger brother, Benjamin, with them the next time they came to Egypt. Joseph leaves the room, and at this moment the Torah provides us with a penetrating insight into his brothers' feelings. They confer with each other, no doubt in a state of great fear, but instead of discussing strategy together, they say to one another:

*Aval asheymim anachnoo al achinoo:*
"Alas, we are so guilty on account of our brother, because we looked on at his anguish, yet paid no heed as he pleaded with us."

Their guilt at having sold Joseph into slavery is so intense and so all-pervasive that, after so many years, their first reaction to a crisis is the belief that this must be a punishment for what they did to Joseph.

We all have our times of guilt, feelings that never seem to leave us.

Jacob must have been plagued by yet another feeling as he fled from his home. He was going to a foreign land, to an uncle whom he had never met, to a world of strangers, and he must have been filled with anxiety and uncertainty about his future.

Do we not, in our own lives, experience the same kind of feelings?

When a young person goes off to college for the first time, he wonders, "Will I make it?" "Will I manage?" When a couple is getting married, deeply in love, doesn't each one silently wonder, "Did I make the right choice?" When a person decides to change his work in the middle of his career, he asks himself, "Am I making a mistake? Will the new career really be better?"

There are many times when each of us feels Jacob's feeling of anxiety about our own future.

What is it that helped Jacob to emerge from his mood of despair? The Torah tells us that he went to sleep and dreamed a wonderful dream. In his dream he saw a ladder standing on the ground, expressing his own despair that he himself was at the bottom rung of that ladder. But that remarkable ladder had another quality. Its top reached to the very heavens. From this great dream, Jacob learned that even when a person descends to the depths of despair, he must always keep alive the vision and the dream of overcoming his difficulties, and with that vision he can go on living.

Each one of us needs that same kind of vision and dream to help us ascend the ladder of life from the lowest rungs to which we are sometimes thrust. Parents who are lonely when a child goes off to school have to retain the vision of the wonderful times they shared together as the child grew. They have to remind themselves of the great experiences yet to come when the child marries, when grandchildren are born. They have to comfort themselves with the knowledge that a successful parent is one who can give his child the strength to grow up and grow away.

When a husband or wife have lost their spouses, the one who remains must recall the beautiful memories of the past, the great moments, both sad and happy, which they shared together. They must retain a vision of a life yet to be lived, of great causes to be joined, of important projects to be accomplished, of the many possibilities of study, of work, of voluntary activities, of the many who still need them and all that they have to offer.

The elderly parent must learn not to rely on children but to constantly work to create other associations through Golden Age groups, through volunteer work for the Temple, for a hospital, for a school.

As I was writing this sermon, I received a call from a lady who is a coordinator for the American Cancer Society. She told me that there is a great need for volunteers from our congregation who will drive a woman to the Beth Israel Hospital for radiation therapy. There are so many opportunities to do *mitzvot*.

And what shall we do when we are weighed down by the burden of guilt which constantly oppresses us? Judaism offers to each one of us the great gift of *teshuvah*, of repentance, of change. It says that none of us is ever hopeless in our relationships to each other. We can make amends to those whom we have wronged. We can ask another person for forgiveness. If another person asks us for forgiveness, Judaism says we must forgive that person. We have no right to go on being angry for the rest of our lives.

Our Tradition says that we can really change ourselves. The next time we are about to lash out at someone with a biting remark, let us stop ourselves. If we stop ourselves often enough, we may find ourselves hurting others far less, and we may find that we are engaged in the slow and painful process of changing ourselves. All this can happen so long as we retain a vision of ourselves of becoming better people, more understanding, more patient, more forgiving people.

And at those times, when we are uncertain about the future, how shall we sustain ourselves? The young person who is going off to college needs to remind himself that if he managed in high school, he will manage in college, too. He will make friends there as he did before. The couple who are getting married wondering if they are making the right choice can help assure the future of their marriage by determining that it shall be a permanent relationship by working hard to see that it does not fail, by recognizing that there is no perfect marriage, and that marriage does not provide instant gratification. But if a couple love each other, their marriage can bring them great fulfillment and strength.

The person who changes his work in the middle of a career because of his dissatisfaction with his previous work must realize that no decision is irrevocable. A person must make a living but each person has a right and a need to find the kind of work which will bring him more gratification and make life more livable. We can face the uncertainties of life so long as we retain the vision of the possibility of self-fulfillment, despite the defeats or disappointments we may suffer along the way.

Do you remember what happened when Jacob awoke from his dream? He said:

*Ayn zeh ki im beit elohim:*
"This is none other than the House of God"

*v'zeh shaar hashamayim:*
"and this is the gate of Heaven."

Jacob discovered the lesson that each of us needs to learn. Regardless of the harshness of the past, regardless of the uncertainty of the future, so long as a person retains the vision of a better future, wherever he is, may become for him "the gateway to heaven."

# 8.
# Impossible Dreams

Recently, Gilbert Kaplan gave a very unusual party. He invited 2700 very important people, family, friends, bankers, corporation heads, and advertisers in his magazine, *Institutional Investor*. First, he invited them to dinner at the Grand Ballroom of the New York Hilton Hotel. What made the party even more unusual than the large number of guests was that after dinner he invited them to join him at Lincoln Center where he conducted the American Symphony Orchestra and the Westminster Symphonic Choir in a performance of Mahler's *Resurrection* Symphony, a very difficult symphony to conduct. The party cost him $100,000 and he gave it in honor of his magazine's fifteenth birthday.

What prompted this unusual party? Kaplan explained that he had always dreamed of conducting an orchestra and he finally decided to make it happen. He worked for a whole year studying the composer Gustave Mahler and the art of conducting.

How did he perform as conductor on that evening? Bernard Holland, music critic of *The New York Times*, said: "For a self-admitted amateur trying to negotiate a complicated piece, he could have done a lot worse. One of a conductor's important tools is the good will of his musicians, and they seemed to want to get him through it."

I have a feeling that, like Gilbert Kaplan, many of us have our own private dreams. Perhaps we once studied a musical instrument, such as the piano or violin, and have sometimes dreamed of performing on the concert stage. If we studied dancing, perhaps we once dreamed of becoming a great ballerina. If we have a nice voice, perhaps we have dreamed of singing with an opera company. If we have acted, perhaps we have dreamed of someday starring in a dramatic performance.

Most of us have such dreams but we quickly dismiss them as unrealizable fantasies. But Gilbert Kaplan did not dismiss his dream, and on that memorable evening, by way of explanation for his action, he recited those great words of Robert Frost: "Two roads diverged in a wood, and I—I took the one less travelled by, and that has made all the difference."

Kaplan was subsequently invited to give the commencement address to the 1983 Class of Westminster Choir College, in Princeton, New Jersey. In his talk about fulfilling dreams, he said: "Dreams come true after hours. Thomas Edison once said that 'Genius is one percent inspiration and ninety-nine percent perspiration.' The world of dreams is not an eight-hour work day but requires continuously going into overtime."

Kaplan used every spare moment he had to realize his great dream. His guests spoke wistfully about their private dreams and compared their own lack of resolve with his determination. His performance made them think of the things they had been doing in their spare time during the past year, while he was preparing for his concert: attending parties, watching TV, sleeping late, often seeking ways to kill time. Gilbert Kaplan's performance suggests that it may be possible for some of us, with enough tenacity and will, to fulfill our own private dreams as he did.

Gilbert Kaplan's kind of dream is fascinating but short-lived. We also need long-term, lasting dreams that bring us fulfillment not only for a resplendent and brilliant evening but that may require a lifetime of preparation, as in choosing a career for ourselves and deciding to become a writer or a scientist or a computer expert. In order for such dreams to be fulfilled, we need many years of study, hard work, even drudgery, and the ability to defer immediate gratification in order to achieve an important goal. But given that kind of determination, it is possible to fulfill such long-term dreams, not only when we are young but even in our older years.

Last year Jacob Landers graduated from New York University Law School, at age sixty-nine. He had been a French teacher, a junior high school principal, then an assistant superintendent in the New York City public schools. As assistant superintendent, he was at first in charge of integration, then he supervised those programs which were paid for by federal and state aid. Both of these jobs were difficult and demanding. He loved his last job best but he was working twelve-to-fifteen-hour days.

In 1968 he suffered a heart attack and almost died. During his recuperation he wrote a doctoral thesis and received his doctorate from New York University. In 1972 he retired from the school system. During his so-called retirement, he taught at Pace University. He explained: "It never occurred to me to retire." In 1975 he underwent a quadruple bypass operation. He recuperated, went back to work, but found himself feeling restless. In 1978, at Thanksgiving dinner, he looked across the table at his daughter, who was going to law school while raising two children, and decided if she could do it, he could, too. Three days later he called New York University Law School and asked if they would admit a person at age sixty-six. The answer he received was: "Certainly, why not?" The following week he took the law board exams, and in September he enrolled at the Law School.

When Jacob Landers was a student in junior high school, he had written in his memory book that he wanted to be a lawyer, but like many other boys who came of age in 1929 his ideas shifted from dreams to solvency: "When I was graduated from Brooklyn College in 1933, it was just in the middle of the Depression. Things looked pretty dim, and I took the first job I could get—teaching. I dismissed law school the way you would dismiss an illusion." His determination to receive a law degree and then to practice law came from a feeling of outrage at discovering that, at his age, people expected him to sit on the sidelines of life. He protested: "You are expected at my age to do whatever you want, as long as it has no impact on the world, to fill time instead of to use it. I hate it."

Jacob Landers refused to be discarded. Instead he fulfilled a lifelong dream, stemming from a determination not to let life pass him by but to use his ability to continue to make an impact on life and on those around him.

There is one more dream each of us needs, a dream to be able to make some contribution to our world. We can make a contribution to the world in so many different ways: through *tzedakah*—by giving to causes that will outlive us, which bring help and healing to those who need it most. We can make a contribution through our own family, through our influence on our children by the values we teach them, through the example we provide for them. We can make a contribution through our personal concern for a neighbor who is bereaved, for a person who is ill, for the kind of person to whom nobody else ever pays any attention. We can make a contribution through investing our energy by working on a problem in our community, or our country, or even on a problem that faces all of humanity.

There is a policeman in Harwich, Massachusetts, whose name is Donald Moreland. A little over a year ago, while on a midnight shift, he heard a newscast about a new arms technology and he recalls: "I suddenly had a feeling that I was a passenger hurtling toward almost certain self-destruction." For several months he brooded about the perils of war. Finally, he decided on a plan. He began a campaign to designate April 6 as World Peace Day, and he appealed to all the nations of the United Nations to "participate in a brief exercise of humanity" in which "the official policy of your government will be not to initiate the taking of human life for a period of twenty-four hours."

Moreland was joined in this campaign by another police officer and a police dispatcher in Wellfleet. They sent letters to the Secretary General of the United Nations and to all the ambassadors of 154 member nations. In the next three weeks, Officer Moreland received an education on how the world resists reform. Everywhere, including our own White House, he encountered red tape, bureaucracy, and resistance to his idea. He was told that he had to go through the proper channels, that he needed to approach the appropriate authorities, and that things could not be done in such a short time.

He did receive a modest response. Governor Dukakis proclaimed April 6 as World Peace Day in Massachusetts. The fourth grade at the Centerville Elementary School held a peace vigil and the students promised to try not to fight on the playground that day. The Harwich Selectmen proclaimed April 6 as World Day of Peace in Harwich. Officer Moreland and his associates spent $300 of their own money on postage and expenses for his unsuccessful campaign. What was his reaction to his lack of success? He said: "I'm eternally optimistic. I'm still convinced that we are autonomous and discrete entities and our input does count, and one man can make a difference."

Does Donald Moreland sound hopelessly naive? Perhaps. And yet, at times, it is because of such "impossible dreams" that the world moves forward, if only an inch or two. And who knows, perhaps one day enough of the Donald Morelands of the world may yet impel the rest of us to create a world where people will devote their energies and resources to establishing peace instead of to plotting annihilation.

Each of us needs some of Donald Moreland's spirit, a spirit expressed so well by that wonderful song: "To dream the impossible dream; to fight the unbeatable foe; to reach when your arms are too weary; to run where the brave dare not go; to right the unrightable wrong. This is my quest, to follow that star no matter how hopeless, no matter how far."

# 9.
# Where Are Our Treasures?

In the city of Cracow, Poland, there once lived a man named Rabbi Isaac, son of Rabbi Yehiel. One night he had a strange dream in which someone told him to go to Prague, where he would find a great treasure under a bridge which leads to the king's palace. When the dream recurred a second and third time, Rabbi Isaac prepared for the journey and set out for Prague.

When he arrived in Prague he found the bridge, but it was guarded day and night and he did not dare dig for the treasure. Nevertheless he went to the bridge every morning and kept walking around it until evening. Finally, the captain of the guard, who had been watching him, asked him in a kindly way whether he was looking for something or waiting for someone. Whereupon Rabbi Isaac told him of the dream which brought him there.

The captain laughed and said, "Poor foolish man. Because of a dream you wore out your shoes to come here. Why, if I had faith in dreams, I would have had to listen to a silly dream which I myself have been having! I have been dreaming that a voice keeps telling me to go to the city of Cracow to dig for treasure under the stove in the house of a Jew by the name of Isaac, son of Yehiel. Can you imagine what it would be like to try to find a man with that name in the city of Cracow?"

Whereupon Rabbi Isaac bade farewell to the captain, traveled home, dug up the treasure from under the stove in his house, and built a House of Prayer with the treasure he had uncovered.

That story has great meaning for each of us because all too often we have the illusion that our greatest treasures are far away. We are constantly looking for new places to see, for more exotic places to visit, for more unusual modes of transportation. We want to travel to the four corners of the earth; we have the feeling that the farther we go, the more happiness we will achieve.

Some of us are fascinated by and envious of the way other people live. We read avidly about stars of screen and TV, about famous athletes, about the meanderings of the jet set and the philandering of the "beautiful people." By contrast, we see our own lives as drab and uninteresting.

Some of us think that happiness lies in our bank vaults, our securities, our savings, our investments, and we dream of how much more we would love to deposit there.

Some people feel that happiness comes from the precious stones we acquire, the diamonds, emeralds, pearls; others, from the furs we wear, the minks, sables, chinchillas; still others, from the cars we drive, the Cadillacs, Lincolns, Mercedes!

Some of our young people believe that they will find true faith in religions other than their own, in Zen Buddhism, in Hare Krishna, in Jews for Jesus.

But the story of Isaac, son of Yehiel, teaches that our greatest treasures are not in Prague under a bridge far away from us. Our greatest treasures are near at hand, beneath the hearth of every home, treasures that we usually take for granted.

What are our greatest treasures?

First, our own families. In a home where a husband and wife can laugh and cry together, can confide in each other, can create an environment of love and warmth together—is there any greater treasure or any greater happiness?

In a home where parents and children can commiserate with each other, where parents and children respect and love each other, where parents and children at times cause each other grief and yet at times also bring each other the greatest pleasure and *naches*—these are our treasures.

Our greatest treasures are close by, not only in our families but in our friends. To know that when you need help, there are some people you can depend upon unconditionally—what a treasure and comfort that is. To know that there is somebody to whom you can pour out your heart, who will listen to you, empathize with you, and understand your feelings—that is a precious gift. To know that there are people whom you can invite to your *simcha* and they will come to join you, regardless of the distance; to know that they will enjoy your *simcha* as much as you will because they are not jealous of you, because your *simcha* is also theirs—what a blessing that is. To know that there is somebody with whom you can be yourself, without pretense, without sham, without masks—that is the treasure of friendship, a treasure that is very close at hand.

We Jews have yet another treasure which we sometimes neglect but one that is also very close by. It is our Faith and our Tradition. We have a great Torah that teaches us how to live as decent human beings, that gives us the kind of permanent values that do not change regardless of the blandishments of a new morality or a new *meshugas* that our society embraces. We have a Tradition that gives us a *Shabbat* and a *Yom Tov*, that takes our ordinary lives of running, chauffeuring, competing, and struggling and transforms us into children of kings, prophets, and sages. These are the opportunities afforded us by our Tradition to celebrate moments of beauty, warmth, and grandeur together with our families, fellow Jews throughout the world and throughout history.

We have a faith that forever challenges us to improve ourselves and to improve our world; a faith that enhances life's joys and gives us the strength to endure life's tragedies; a faith that teaches that a Jew never despairs.

What a treasure we possess and how close at hand it can be if we choose to discover it and use it.

There is a legend about an artist who became very dissatisfied with his work and decided he would only be happy if he could paint the most beautiful object in the world. He traveled far and wide to find this object. One day he stopped a bride on the way to her wedding and asked, "Tell me, what is the most beautiful thing in the world?"

Without hesitation, she answered, "Love."

So the artist tried to paint love, but his efforts were to no avail. Then he saw a soldier returning from war and he asked him the same question: "What is the most beautiful thing in the world?"

The soldier answered, "The most beautiful thing in the world is peace."

Whereupon the artist tried to paint peace, but somehow the result was very poor. Then he met a holy man reciting prayers and asked him the same question. The holy man answered, "The most beautiful thing in the world is faith."

The artist tried to paint faith but again was unsuccessful.

Finally, he returned to his home, tired and dejected. His wife greeted him joyously and he saw in her eyes the love of which the bride had spoken. He sat down on his favorite chair in the living room, looked about him, and suddenly felt the peacefulness of which the soldier had spoken. He took his children in his lap and in their eyes he beheld the faith of which the holy man had spoken. And suddenly, the artist realized that he had found what he had been seeking, not somewhere far away but in the intimacy and love of his own home and his own family.

Our greatest treasures are very near at hand.

# 10.
# Why We Are Ungrateful

An unfortunate human trait most of us share is that we are often ungrateful to those who give us the most, and this seems to hold true of all our relationships.

For example, when our children are infants, we nurture them. When they go to school, we chauffeur them. When they go to college, we work hard to pay their tuition and board. And when they go out on a date and come home late, we find it difficult to fall asleep until we hear the front door open. Yet when we ask our children to cut the grass, or to do the laundry, or to perform that most insurmountable of tasks—to clean their room—we are often met with the response: "I don't have the time," or "Why do you always pester me and drive me crazy?" And if our child does miraculously comply with our request, he will perform the task with a maddening slowness so that often we end up doing it ourselves.

We ask ourselves: why are they so ungrateful? We do everything for them, why are they so unwilling to reciprocate even a little bit?

We are often ungrateful to those who give us the most.

This is true of parents' relationships to children as well. Children are constantly giving parents great gifts to which the parents are often indifferent. Children provide us with the gift of a new life, with the opportunity to guide, to teach, to see an infant grow from helplessness to adulthood, to see a child develop from dependence to maturity. Children provide us with the gift of posterity, the hope that perhaps they will not only carry on in the path we have charted for them but that they will improve upon our pattern of life and become even better people than we are. Our children provide us with the gift of keeping us young. (At times they also give us gray hair.) But because they are a part of a new generation, they present a constant challenge to our own ideas and traditions. We have to meet this challenge by remaining alert to new ideas, by being able to discuss these ideas with our children, by teaching them and learning from them at the same time.

Our children bring us many gifts, and often we are unaware of how much meaning they add to our lives.

What of the relationship of a husband and wife, who see each other at their worst, in moments of anger, frustration, and despair. Yet if there is real love between them, they are able to help each other more than anybody else in the world. They can strengthen and encourage each other in the face of life's greatest difficulties. So many of us discover that without this sharing of life, life itself can become unbearable. Yet how rarely do we give expression to the gratefulness we should feel to those who give us most.

Why are we so ungrateful to those who give us so much? Why are we so often angry, resentful, and hostile to one another? Perhaps it is because in every household and in every family there are the inevitable stresses and strains that create conflict and friction, with their accompanying arguments and fights. It is unrealistic to believe that any household is conducted in a constant state of bliss, where people live on a constant plane of perpetual gratefulness to each other.

But perhaps there is another reason why we are ungrateful to those who give us so much. Perhaps it is because we resent so deeply our dependency on each other. The fact that a child knows that he is so dependent on his parents for so long, that without his parents he cannot survive, or grow, or receive an education, or become an adult; to always be at the receiving end of somebody else's largesse, even one's own parents, is to fill a person with resentment at the awareness of his own dependency and helplessness.

Maybe an even more important reason why we are ungrateful to those who give us so much is our tendency to take each other for granted. As a result, we seem to appreciate only what we have lost.

When do we appreciate parents most? When they are no longer with us. We use their expressions in our speech, we think back to their love and their wisdom, we feel guilty that we didn't call them or write them or see them more often.

When do we appreciate children most? When the "nest is empty" and the house becomes unbearably quiet. We look into their rooms and ask ourselves: "Where did the years fly? Why was I always so busy with *narishkeitin* instead of spending more time with them? Why didn't I realize that those years were the greatest years?"

When do we appreciate a husband or wife most? It is when one is gone and we feel utterly lost without the other, when we can no longer share the small talk, the experiences, great and small, the beauties of life and its sorrows, when we have the feeling that there is nobody to talk to, nobody who really knows how to listen to us, nobody who cares whether we come home at night.

Perhaps the reason we are ungrateful is because we take each other for granted while we are together.

How can we solve this perennial problem of being ungrateful to those who give us so much? This is precisely the purpose of today's Torah reading. Moses says to the children of Israel, when you come to The Promised Land and gather the harvest of the land, do not forget the Constant Giver of all bounties. Bring the first fruits of your harvest to the Sanctuary and present them as an offering to God. The verse says:

*V'amarta eylav:*
"You shall say to the priest . . ."

And Rashi interpolates this comment:

*Sheeyncha kfui tovah:*
"Say to him that you are not an ingrate . . ."

that you are aware of the blessings that God has given you, and that you have come to give thanks for His gifts.

Once the Israelites would be settled on their own land, working hard and seeing the fruits of their labor, how easy it would be to forget the God who inspired them to come to this land, who gave them the strength to till its fields. How easy it would be instead to begin to believe that they were self-made people, that they owed nothing to anybody. Therefore, the Torah says, as soon as you harvest your fields, bring the *bikkurim*, the first fruits, to the Sanctuary lest you become ungrateful, lest you take the gifts of your life for granted.

For the same reason our Tradition developed a wonderful system of *b'rachot*, blessings. According to the Talmud, a Jew should say at least *meah b'rachot*, one hundred blessings, each day. When he opens his eyes, he should say: *"Baruch Attah . . . pokeyach ivrim"*—Thank God I can see. When he arises from bed, he should say: *"zokeyf k'fufim"*—Thank God I can stand up. When he eats a piece of bread, he should say: *"hamotzi lechem min haaretz"*—Thank God for providing me with bread and sustenance. There is a blessing to be said upon first seeing trees in blossom, for putting on a new article of clothing, for eating a new fruit, upon seeing a great scholar. This is our Tradition's way of cultivating an attitude of gratefulness in us, to teach us to say a blessing for each of our gifts: for our parents, who love us and care for us; for our children, who challenge us and keep us young; for the husband and wife, who sustain each other; for the ability to work, study, create, hope, love, and be alive each day.

We humans have a proclivity for being ungrateful. Therefore, our Tradition says, train yourself to be constantly aware of your blessings, and give thanks for them each day of your life.

The poet, Joseph Auslander, expressed this thought so beautifully when he wrote:

> Lord, I would thank You for these things:
>    Not sunlight only, but sullen rain;
> Not only laughter with lifted wings,
>    But the heavy muted hands of pain.
>
> Lord, I would thank You for so much:
>    The toil, no less than the well-earned ease;
> The glory always beyond our touch
>    That bows the head and bends the knees.
>
> Lord, there are gifts of brighter gold
>    Than deepest mine or mint can yield:
> Friendship and love and a dream to hold,
>    The look that heartened, the word that healed.
>
> Lord, I would thank You for eyes to see
>    Miracles in our everyday earth:
> The colors that crowd monotony,
>    The flame of the humblest flower's birth.
>
> Lord, I would thank You for gifts without season:
>    The flash of a thought like a banner unfurled,
> The splendor of faith and the sparkle of reason,
>    The tolerant mind in a turbulent world!

# 11.
# Achieving Perspective

On *Sukkot* the major symbols of the Festival present a striking paradox. They remind us of "the worst of times and the best of times."

The *sukkah* reminds us of the "worst of times." It reminds us of our bondage in Egypt, followed by the sojourn in the desert, when we suffered all kinds of setbacks and defeats.

But then we have a set of different symbols, which remind us of the "best of times." The *etrog, lulav, hadasim,* and *aravot* remind us of the time that our people finally settled in the Promised Land and they gathered in these symbols of the harvest as well as all the other bounties of the land.

Why should our Tradition provide us with these symbols on the same Holy Day which seem to represent opposite poles of human experience?

Perhaps, indeed, this was done for a special reason: to teach us that both kinds of symbols are needed as a symbolic representation of the reality of Jewish history and that both have very important teachings for our people.

What are these very different symbols supposed to teach us as a people? The reason for the *sukkah* is given by the Torah in these words:

> *L'maan yedu doroteychem ki vasukkot hoshavti et b'nai yisrael*
> *b'hotzii otam meyeretz mitzrayim:*
> "So that your generations may know that I made the children of Israel to dwell in *sukkot*, when I brought them out of the land of Egypt."

As Israel settled in its own land, built homes, and acquired fields, the Torah recognized the likelihood of our people becoming smug, self-satisfied, and even arrogant. Therefore, God commands: leave your beautiful homes and dwell in a little *sukkah*, at least for a week, because this is how you began; you were not always so fancy and so comfortable as you are now. The purpose of this temporary dwelling was to inculcate greater understanding and compassion for those who continue to live in substandard houses and in slums, who are constantly exposed to the hazards and uncertainties of a life of poverty and deprivation.

It is very hard, when we live in a luxurious home, drive a beautiful car, and can afford the basic necessities and even many luxuries, to remember what it was like for us or our parents who did not live this way and what it must be like for people who still live this way. If we complain about inflation and the recession, how devastating these must be to those who have been struggling to subsist even before our economy fell into such deep trouble.

*Basukkot teyshvu:*
"Dwell in a *sukkah* so you shall be reminded of those who still live in *sukkot.*"

And what are the four symbols of the harvest, the *etrog, lulav, hadasim,* and *aravot*, supposed to teach us? We say a blessing over them: *"al n'tilat lulav."* During the Hallel Service we wave them in all directions to symbolize that our blessings from God come to us from every direction. All this is intended to teach us to be grateful to God for all our blessings: for life, our families, our homes, our health, our Synagogue, and our faith.

I imagine you must know some people who are constant complainers. In Yiddish we say about such a person: *Er burchet*—he grumbles and complains. Or, we say: *Er hot a farkrimten ponim*—his face is always contorted. Some people complain about everything: their family, their wife, their husband, their parents, or their children. In upstate New York, long before the John Birch Society appeared as an organization, a Rabbi described a whole group of men who sat in the back of his *Shul* as *burchers,* who would complain about him and about everything else! The lesson of the *etrog* and *lulav* is that you are surrounded by blessings and don't even know it.

Every *b'racha* prescribed by our Tradition is to remind you of a blessing you possess: when you open your eyes in the morning, give thanks for the gift of sight. When you stand up from bed, be grateful that you can get up and go to work. Look around you and give thanks that you are part of a family who care about you and love you. It's time to stop complaining and to begin to appreciate the gifts that are yours each day of your life.

The *etrog* and *lulav*, symbols of the harvest, are intended to teach us one more lesson. Again, in the words of the Torah:

> *Uvkutzrechem et ktzir artzechem:*
> "When you reap the harvest of your land, you shall not wholly reap the harvest of your field . . ."

> *Le'ani v'lageyr taazov otam:*
> "You shall leave some of the harvest for the poor and for the stranger . . ."

It is not enough to be understanding of another's plight. You have to be willing to do something about it by sharing your bounties with those who need your help. You have to be willing to give *tzedakah*, for Israel, for those who are hungry in many parts of the world, for those in your own community who feel defeated and hopeless and are ready to give up the struggle for existence.

Like our peoples' experience, each one of us also has our bad times and our good times. We have our hard times when there are struggles, business reverses, defeats, and disappointments. And we also have our good times when we achieve a goal, or receive a promotion, or celebrate a successful accomplishment, or rejoice in a *simcha*.

There are some people who remember only the hard times of the past. They remember the struggles, the disappointments, and the heartbreak of their lives, and their attitude becomes one of bitterness, hostility, and cynicism. They become angry with the world and with people. They say, "Life gave me a raw deal!" They cannot deal with the present because they are crippled by their own anger and hostility.

And there are other people who remember only the good times of the past. They talk about "the good old days," when people were more friendly, when tradespeople took pride in their work, when kids used to listen to their parents. Life was simpler then and made much more sense, they say. As a result, they view today's people and events with a jaundiced eye. They say that the kids will never amount to anything, living is becoming impossible, and the world is rapidly going to hell.

The symbols of the Festival of *Sukkot* remind us of the need for a balanced view, for perspective. Life is a mixture for all of us. *Basukkot teshvu* reminds us of its struggles, hardships, problems, and defeats. But at the same time, the *etrog, lulav, hadasim,* and *aravot* remind us of our harvest of blessings: of our accomplishments, our *naches*, our *simchas*, the beautiful moments, and even occasionally, of great triumphs.

When a person achieves this kind of perspective, then he can truly fulfill the great *mitzvah* of this Festival:

> *Usmachtem lifney hashem elokeychem:*
> "You shall rejoice before your God."

The person who can become a genuinely great human being is one who is happy with his own life and grateful for his blessings and at the same time is concerned about the needs and the happiness of other human beings as well.

May the beautiful symbols of *Sukkot* remind us that each of us needs to achieve this perspective in our own lives.

# 12.
# A Sense of Perspective

If Shakespeare is right that there are "sermons in stories," how much more true is it that there are "sermons" in the lives of human beings.

I read an article recently in *The New York Times* by Dave Anderson about the football star Jim Plunkett, and I was very moved to read about his family background and his resultant attitude to life. Jim Plunkett is the quarterback who led the Oakland Raiders to the Super Bowl, and after his team won, he was selected as the most valuable player in the National Football League. His own personal triumph was even greater, because after being released by the San Francisco 49ers, he was unemployed for two seasons, and everybody thought he was finished in football. When Oakland hired him, they did so as a third string quarterback, hoping that he still had a little potential left in him, which might justify their investment. When the Oakland quarterback Don Pastorini was injured, they called on Jim Plunkett to take his place, and he led the team to victory in the Super Bowl.

It's a great story, a defeat and a triumph, but both failure and success are very difficult for most people to handle because either one can destroy a person. Jim Plunkett has a rare quality which has sutained him till now, a sense of perspective. That is why failure didn't cripple him with a feeling of hopelessness and that is the same reason he will probaby be able to handle success without losing his sense of balance.

He achieved a sense of perspective from his parents and the kind of home they created. He and his two older sisters were raised by parents who were both blind. His father was legally blind from birth. He wore very thick glasses but he could see a little. His mother had sight until she was twenty years old, when she developed scarlet fever. After that, she became totally blind. They met each other at a school for the blind in San Jose. When you grow up in a house where both parents are blind, you develop a sense of perspective about what's important and what is not.

Jim and his mother would take long walks together during which she would ask him to describe the scenery to her. He describes those walks: "Especially in the parks. She always wanted to know what the trees and hills looked like. We took a lot of walks because neither of my parents could drive."

It's a way of achieving perspective about the beauty of God's universe that most of us ignore because we are sighted. That is the reason our Tradition has created such marvelous blessings, to remind us to thank God for the beauty with which He has enveloped us. When you see a lofty mountain, or a vast desert, or a falling star, or a lightning flash, you say a blessing: *"Baruch atta adonay eloheynoo melech haolam oseh maasey brayshit"*—Blessed are you, Lord our God, King of the Universe, who has created nature's great phenomena.

When you see a beautiful tree or a beautiful animal, there is a special blessing: *"Baruch atta adonay eloheynoo melech haolam shekacha lo b'olamo"*—Blessed are you, Lord our God, King of the Universe, who has created such creatures in His universe.

When you see a tree blossoming in the spring, you utter a blessing: *"Baruch atta adonay eloheynoo melech haolam shelo chiseyr b'olamo davar"*—Blessed are you, Lord our God, who has omitted nothing from His universe—*"oovara vo b'riyot tovot v'ilanot tovim"*—who has created beautiful creatures and beautiful trees—*"lehanot bahem b'ney adam"*—to bring pleasure to human beings.

To achieve a sense of perspective about life, you have to give yourself time to see the beauty that surrounds you.

Jim Plunkett learned something else from his parents. As he tells it: "One parent always was taking care of the other. My mother would tell us kids to take care of our father. And our father would tell us to take care of our mother. My father, and later on, my sisters, prepared most of the meals. My father wouldn't let my mother cook. He didn't want her to get burned on the stove."

Jim Plunkett learned from his parents how to create a good marriage with the kind of love that brings with it devotion and concern for one another. There are so many marriages which are foundering today because people are so concerned about themselves that they have little room left for their spouse. People today speak about the importance of *my* career and *my* growth, *my* needs and *my* feelings, the fulfillment of *my* personality and *my* potential. The result is that nobody is thinking of the other person's needs and feelings. Nobody is thinking of the hard work that is necessary to create a shared relationship which should satisfy some of the needs of both partners but which also requires sacrifices and the ability to give on the part of each partner.

One of the beautiful Hebrew words for love is *hibah*. It comes from the same root as the Hebrew word *hovah*, meaning commitment and obligation. A real marriage can only be created by two people who seek not only their own gratification but are equally concerned that the person they love should also find fulfillment.

It requires a sense of perspective.

There was another quality that Jim learned from his parents. They possessed a spirit of determination that they were going to lead normal lives, regardless of how difficult the obstacles. Plunkett says about his parents: "My parents were very stubborn. If they wanted to go somewhere, they went. Or if they wanted to clean the house, they cleaned the house. When my room was a mess, my mother always knew. I was supposed to make my bed, but if I didn't, she'd walk in and feel the bed to see if I had. And if I left some clothes on the floor, she would step on them and find out. She always knew." He continued: ". . . one of the things that always annoyed my parents was having others thinking they were handicapped. I remember them saying that they weren't handicapped, that they could do just about anything except see." His father died a number of years ago but Jim is reminded of this quality whenever he visits his mother. "Even at my age," he said with a laugh, "when I walk in and hug her, she reaches for the top of my head and feels the hair in the back to see if I need a haircut." That spirit of determination of his parents, their refusal to see themselves as handicapped, gave a sense of perspective to their children.

There is a new phrase which is very popular today; I hear it all the time. A person says, "I can't handle it." If there is a problem in the family, someone inevitably says, "I can't handle it." A child may be having a problem with a teacher and somebody says, "I can't handle it." If there is illness in the family, someone says, "I can't handle it." That phrase is usually accompanied by a corollary phrase which is, "You take care of it." And it's usually accompanied by a gesture: reaching for a valium.

We need a sense of perspective like the one Jim Plunkett's parents had. With their determination, they somehow managed to handle a marriage, work, children, and love. We can do the same and we can do it without valium.

I marvel at what upsets people. Some cry about a scratch on the car. Some are perturbed by a salesperson who is unfriendly. Some are enraged if the car in front of them doesn't move precisely at the moment the light changes.

Perspective means the capacity to view things in their relative importance. Jim Plunkett learned perspective from his parents and so can we.

Perspective means to be grateful each day for the gift of life and the beauty of the universe which God has created for you and me.

Perspective means to work hard at the relationships which count most in our life, with a spouse, a child, a parent, to expect to give as well as to receive.

Perspective means to cultivate the conviction that nothing in life can ever defeat us, neither illness, disappointment, nor failure, as long as our spirit and determination remain strong, undaunted, and unafraid.

# 13.
# Be a *Mentch*

At a recent conference for child care professionals, the renowned psychologist, Dr. Jerome Bruner, cautioned all parents with these words: "... I think parents should forget the genius bit—what you want is a human being, a *Mentch*, not a genius."

I liked his use of that term *Mentch*. For Jews, the word conjures up a whole host of associations and ideas, all of them adding up to the meaning: a great human being.

Some years ago, I was told a story by a good friend and distinguished colleague, Rabbi Max Routtenberg, past President of the Rabbinical Assembly. When he was a young boy growing up in Montreal, his grandfather used to study Talmud with him each day after school. The lad's attention was often distracted by a scene taking place across the street and he kept looking out of the window. He saw his friends playing ball and would have wanted to join them. In desperation his grandfather would say to him, *"Moshe, Moshe, ver veist tzv du vest amol zein a Mentch"*—Moshe, Moshe, who knows if you'll ever become a *Mentch*.

In this context, a *Mentch* means the kind of person who will appreciate learning, and Torah, and the study of God's word. I can assure you that Rabbi Routtenberg's grandfather would be very happy to see the kind of wonderful *Mentch* his grandson became.

When a Jewish parent was displeased by his child's behavior, he would express the hope that *Er vet zich noch amol oismentshlen*—He'll yet become a human being! He will become civilized one day, we mustn't despair.

When a person failed to perform the basic acts demanded by an elemental sense of decency, it was a source of shock and consternation and one asked about such a person, *"Avoo iz zein mentchlichkeit?"*—What happened to his humanity?

About a person who was petty and mean-spirited, it was explained, *Er iz doch a klein mentchele*—He is a spiritual pygmy—what can you expect from such a person?

Some of our associations with the word *Mentch* are incorporated in the folk wisdom of proverbs, and I would like to share several of them with you. Our people knew the reality of human imperfection and, therefore, they said: "*A mentch iz nit kein malach*"—A person is not an angel. Even the best of us is frail and weak and we often sin and make mistakes.

You recall how our patriach Jacob deceived his blind father, Isaac, in order to acquire his brother's birthright. He committed a great sin, which the Torah does not attempt to hide. Ultimately, he engaged in a mysterious struggle with an angel. Jacob was victorious in that struggle but he emerged from the battle limping. Perhaps the meaning of that battle is that Jacob had to struggle with himself to overcome his own sinfulness. He had to struggle to become a *Mentch* and he did not emerge unscathed.

A *Mentch iz nit kein malach*—a *Mentch* is not an angel. We Jews do not expect perfection of any person, even of one who becomes a real *Mentch*, but each of us must enter the fray to try to become a *Mentch*.

Now, we may not expect perfection but, on the other hand, we Jews have a special aversion to cruelty. If you want to describe a person who is heartless, you say, *Dos Mentch fun ihm hot zich aroysgetzoygen*"—The *Mentch* in him has disappeared.

Did you see the story in the *Boston Globe* recently about the treatment accorded a blind teacher in Pittsburgh? Ceinwen King-Smith, thirty-five years old, graduated Phi Beta Kappa from Stanford University. She received a Master's Degree from Harvard and taught in private schools for ten years. She had to go to Federal Court to obtain a job in the Pittsburgh public schools. In the Junior High School where she teaches, students throw spitballs at her. They have stolen money from her purse. They tie her shoes together when she comes near a student's desk. She spends many hours removing chewing gum wads from her hair. Last month, the school board suspended her with pay. They want to dismiss her because of the disciplinary problems in her class. She argues that she should be reinstated with a full-time aide to help her control the students. The case is still pending.

What kind of people are those at her school and on that school board? Why don't they suspend the students for their cruelty to a human being? One can only conclude that for such people *Dos Mentch fun zei hot zich aroysgetzoygen*—The *Mentch* has simply disappeared from their midst.

There is another beautiful proverb about a *Mentch*. It says: *A Mentch iz alemol a Mentch*—A *Mentch* remains a mentch under all circumstances. Such a person can be relied upon to do the right thing wherever he may be.

Rabbi Leo Baeck was a distinguished Reform rabbi in Berlin before the Second World War. In 1938 and 1939, when he was almost seventy years old, he was offered the pulpit of a large congregation in Cincinnati. But he refused to leave his people in Germany. He made many trips between Berlin and London to make arrangements for German Jewish children to stay in Britain. Ultimately, he was imprisoned by the Nazis in the concentration camp Theresienstadt. There, by day, he had to drag a garbage cart along the streets. But at night, Rabbi Baeck would give illegal lectures to fellow Jews on philosophy, literature, and Jewish history. In total darkness, some eight hundred to nine hundred people would crowd into the attic of a barracks to listen to his teaching. In the midst of hunger, disease, and torture, he was able to give courage to his people by teaching them every night. Whenever he could steal a moment from his enforced labor, he would write on tiny scraps of paper what was ultimately to become a profound philosophical history of the Jewish people. He would then read from those scraps of paper to his fellow Jews and thereby give them the will to survive. "A *Mentch* remains a mentch even in Theresienstadt."

Some months ago, a remarkably brilliant man by the name of Robert Kirsch died at the age of fifty-eight. He was the book critic for the *Los Angeles Times*. He wrote more book reviews than any modern critic, six days a week for twenty-three years. In his spare time he also wrote a dozen books, fiction and nonfiction. Robert Kirsch was born in Brooklyn and not too long ago he summed up his career and his values in these words: "In the end, all of it is an attempt to recapture Coney Island and the lesson I learned there: 'Live, read, grow, and be a *Mentch*.' "

That's a beautiful summation of life and he somehow put it all together in seven words. Let me interpret his words for you. *"Live"*— try to live each day fully, enjoy it as a gift, and give thanks for all your blessings.

*"Read"*—don't let TV take you away from reading. Because when you read, you share the lives and insights of the greatest minds that

ever lived. The more you read the great books of Jewish Tradition, the more you become inspired by the greatness of its beauty, truth, and wisdom.

"*Live, read,* and *grow*"—never stop growing as a person; never become satisfied with what you have achieved till now. Let your mind keep growing and stretching with new ideas and insights. Let your heart keep growing with greater sensitivity and understanding for others and their needs. Let your soul keep growing with greater openness to God for the strength and meaning He can give your life.

"*Live, read, grow,* and *be a Mentch.*" Try to be the kind of person who will be respected and loved, not because of your power, fame, or fortune but because you personify the qualities of *Mentchlichkeit*. Because you are fair, generous, and compassionate under all circumstances.

For Robert Kirsch, his words were like a beautiful epitaph for his life. For each of us, his words are a beautiful evocation of the goals and values we need for our own lives.

# 14.
# How to Become a *Mentch*

If you want to write a best-seller, write a book entitled *How to Lose Weight While Eating Ice Cream*, or *How to Look Younger Each Day of Your Life*, or *How to Raise a Genius Without Ever Opening a Book*.

Now, what if somebody decided to write a book entitled *How to Be a* Mentch? I doubt that it would cause a great stir. Nonetheless, that is why you and I are here today on *Rosh Hashanah*. It is to talk about "How to be a *Mentch*," how to become a genuine human being.

*Rosh Hashanah* is an optimistic time for us. It says that each of us can become a *Mentch* through *teshuvah*, or penitence, by changing our lives and becoming better people. Our Tradition recognized that *teshuvah*, or change, is not easy. Most of us fear change; we avoid it; we even fight it. We need help in learning how to do *teshuvah*, how to use change in order to become a real *Mentch*.

The great Hasidic teacher Rabbi Nachman of Bratzlav provided us with a formula for *teshuvah* which each one of us can use in our own lives. He said, "There are three requisites for repentance." The first is "seeing eyes." And, he explains, "Let your eyes see your conduct."

We are often blind to our own failings. We do not see our arrogance as we ask another, "To which college was your child accepted?" The name of the college often determines our attitude to that person and the child. We do not see the harm we do with our short tempers. We become angry and we say terrible things to each other, words that rankle long after the argument is over. We are unaware of our rudeness as we speak to a waiter, a secretary, a stewardess. We are blind to our callousness, our insensitivity to another's feelings, to another's pain.

If we are to change, we need to open our eyes to the failings that demean us and diminish others.

"Seeing Eyes" had another meaning for the Bratzlaver. He explained, "Let your eyes see the blessings which are yours."

A while ago, Dava Sobell, science writer for *The New York Times*, engaged in an experiment of sleep deprivation and isolation for several weeks. She described her reactions in great detail. She was lonely for her husband and her friends. She missed the ability to tell the difference between day and night. She longed to see grass, to look at blossoms on the trees.

"Seeing Eyes" means: Look about you and see the blessings of your family, of parents, a spouse, children, grandchildren. Observe the miracle of day changing into night, and night into day. We have a whole system of beautiful blessings in our Tradition to help us appreciate the beauty and grandeur of life. We even have a blessing when you see the first blossoms on a tree in the spring. It says, *Baruch atta hashem*—Thank you, God—*shelo cheesayr baolamo davar*—who has omitted nothing from His world—*uvarah vo b'reeot tovot v'ilanot tovim lehanot bahem b'nai adam*—and has created beautiful creatures and beautiful trees, to bring pleasure to human beings.

If you want to become a *Mentch*, you have to develop "seeing eyes" in order to appreciate the blessings which surround you.

Rabbi Nachman said there is a second indispensable requisite for becoming a *Mentch*. We need to develop "hearing ears." And he explained, "Let your ears hear words of admonition . . ."

Ours is an age of "doing your own thing." We don't like to be told that we are doing something wrong. Adolescents resent their parents' admonitions and respond by saying, "Don't lay a trip on me." When children live together and parents express their disapproval, the children are likely to retort, "You're way behind the times." When we listen to a sermon, we resent being castigated; or we say, "Boy, did he give it to them!"; or we agree with the preacher and return to our torpor and our indifference. If you want to be a *Mentch*, says Rabbi Nachman, "Let your ears hear words of admonition."

"Hearing ears" has yet another meaning. It means "Listen to the cries of despair that call to you."

Listen to the people in our country today who have lost their jobs and together with their jobs have lost not only their livelihoods but their dignity and their hope for the future.

Listen to the people in our country who have lost their homes and are wandering from state to state, from shelter to shelter, in quest of a job, in a vain search to find a place to settle.

Listen to the children in our country who are hungry and whose school lunch programs have been cut so that they cannot concentrate on study and cannot learn.

"Hearing ears" means listen to those in your society who are in despair and respond to their cries.

Finally, Rabbi Nachman taught that there is a third requisite for changing into a *Mentch*. It is "an understanding heart." And he explained, "Let your heart understand its eternal purpose."

On *Rosh Hashanah* we must ask ourselves: why are we here on this earth? Is it to acquire bigger houses, sleeker cars, to join more exclusive clubs? Is it to accumulate more power, more exciting leisure, greater ways to escape reality?

Rabbi Nachman says, if you want to be a *Mentch*, "Let your heart understand its eternal purpose." Our eternal purpose is *l'takeyn olam b'malchut shaddai*, to improve the universe. Our task is to create a society where every person has a job and dignity and hope. Our responsibility is to create a society where old people and poor people do not die of the heat as they did in our country this summer because they have no air conditioner, sometimes not even a fan. Our purpose is to create a society where each person will have a place to live together with his family. Our obligation is to create a country where children have enough to eat so they can learn and grow and become productive members of our society.

Sometimes we discover "life's purpose" in the most unsuspecting places. The writer Phyllis Theroux tells of a train trip she took with her ten-year-old daughter. The mother had purchased a novel by an acclaimed writer and was planning to read it on the train. She hoped that she might find in it some of the answers to questions which were preoccupying her. She writes, "Everyone wants to leave the world with something more than a cemetery marker, yet how, in what way, for whom and when?"

But her daughter had other plans. This was their first mother-daughter excursion and she wanted to talk with her mother without the interference of her two brothers. The daughter talked to her mother about her future. She said, "I think I want to be either a teacher or at least someone who helps people." Then she told her mother how, in school the previous year, some of the class didn't understand fractions, and the teacher asked her to explain them to her classmates Daniel and Jeremy. Daniel understood but Jeremy didn't, so she had to figure out a different way to explain them. He finally understood and she felt very good. Later, she told her mother about another experience that made her happy. She said, "Like when Justin (her younger brother) hurts himsef on his bike and I fix him up with pillows and band-aids and get him to stop crying. That really makes me feel good inside myself."

The mother wrote that those three hours of discussion were the best time she had spent in a long time. Along the way, her daughter had taught her a great deal about "life's purpose." It is to be of help to another, like a mother listening to her daughter's hopes and dreams, a student helping a classmate to understand fractions, a sister helping to comfort a brother. The child taught her mother that what each of us needs in order to learn the purpose of our lives is "an understanding heart."

A book on *How to Be a Mentch* will probably never make the best-seller list. But it might just contain the most important teachings we will ever learn. It would say that if you cultivate seeing eyes, hearing ears, and an understanding heart, you can become an altogether different person, and, in your own way, you can help to save the world.

# 15.
# Edward Steichen: A Mother's Influence

Sometimes the best sermons are found in the lives of great men. We can learn a great deal from their experiences, from the molding influences that shaped their characters.

Edward Steichen died at the age of ninety-three. He was one of the world's greatest photographers, "who transformed his medium into an art." Each of his photographs was like a beautiful painting.

The first photographs he took were almost his last. In 1895, at the age of sixteen, he bought a Kodak camera with his mother's money. He took fifty pictures, using subjects around his house. When the films were returned by the developer, only one had been clear enough to develop into a picture; the others were a total loss. He recalled the differing reactions of his father and mother. "My father thought one picture out of fifty was a hopeless proposition, but my mother said the picture [of his sister at the piano] was so beautiful and so wonderful that it was worth forty-nine failures."

Because his mother encouraged him, he went on to teach himself photography, ultimately making it his life's vocation.

Sometimes an encouraging word from a parent, a teacher, or a friend can make the difference between despair or faith in oneself, hopelessness or faith in one's potentialities.

The Rabbis said:

*Chachamim hizaharu b'divreychem:*
"Wise men, be careful with your words."

We ought to be so careful in the words we use to each other. Some words can build and strengthen; others may destroy those we love most.

## Living Courageously 61

The beauty of Edward Steichen's creations did not come by chance; they came from long study, experimentation, and preparation. He once took more than one thousand shots of a single cup and saucer, as he experimented with the effects of various lighting arrangements. "It was this infinite pain and the knowledge it produced" that gave his pictures their unique quality.

He took a very famous picture of the sculptor Auguste Rodin. Before taking the photograph, Steichen spent every Saturday for a year studying Rodin as the sculptor worked in his Paris studio, and only when he decided on the composition he wanted, at the end of that year, did he finally bring his camera.

Most of us today seek an instant response in everything we do. When we want instant entertainment, we simply flick the TV switch. When we are hungry, we go to the freezer for instant food. When we are worried or agitated, we take a tranquilizer to achieve instant equanimity. If we have a headache, we seek instant relief by taking an aspirin. We are impatient with the basic requisites of growth and maturation: reading, studying, working, and preparing for a meaningful life and a vocation; facing our problems, struggling with them, and learning to live with them without expecting that every moment in life will bring with it instant bliss.

It was Edward Steichen's hard work, his desire for perfection, and his meticulous preparations that made him the great photographer he was.

In his autobiography, *A Life in Photography*, he told of another instance in which his mother's influence shaped his thinking throughout his life.

> Once, when I was ten years old, I came home from school, and as I was entering the door of her millinery shop, I turned back and shouted into the street, "You dirty little kike!" My mother called me over to the counter where she was serving customers and asked me what it was that I had called out. With innocent frankness, I repeated the insulting remark. She requested the customers to excuse her, locked the door of the shop and took me upstairs to our apartment. There, she talked to me quietly and earnestly for a long, long time, explaining that all people were alike regardless of race, creed, or color. She talked about the evils of bigotry and intolerance.
>
> This was possibly the most important single moment in my growth toward manhood, and it was certainly on that day the

seed was sown, that sixty-six years later grew into an exhibition called "The Family of Man."

What was it about that experience that made such a lasting impression on the mind of the ten-year-old boy? It was certainly the enduring content of her words. But perhaps even more important, it was her willingness to close the store and to send her customers home though she needed the money badly. It was the seriousness with which she viewed her son's manifestation of prejudice.

Each of us can also have a profound influence for good on those we love, on those with whom we associate. But our words and our values become meaningful only to the extent that we ourselves believe in them so completely that we are willing to make real sacrifices on their behalf.

In 1952 Steichen, as director of the Department of Photography for the Museum of Modern Art, traveled to eleven countries in search of material for the "Family of Man" exhibition. In 1955 the exhibition opened and was ultimately viewed by more than nine million people in sixty-nine lands. In book form, *The Family of Man* sold three million copies.

What was its purpose? Edward Steichen explained: "As a mirror of the essential oneness of mankind throughout the world."

What was its source? An afternoon, sixty-six years before, in Hancock, Michigan, when a mother demonstrated her concern at seeing bigotry in her own child.

# 16.
# Fathers and Sons

Anatole Broyard, who is a distinguished book reviewer for *The New York Times*, recently wrote a poignant essay entitled: "The Silent Generations." He began by saying, "I'm sandwiched in silence. My father was not a talker and neither is my son."

First, he describes his father's silence:

> When I was a boy, my father's silence was one of the great mysteries of my life. Not only did he fail to answer when I spoke to him, he didn't even seem to hear me. There was no sign, no flicker in his face, to show that I had spoken and I sometimes wondered whether I actually had. I used to stand there and listen, trying to catch the echo of my voice.
>
> If I could have got my father's eye, could have looked him squarely in the face, I might have compelled him to answer me, or at least to acknowledge that I had spoken, but it was impossible to do this because he had a way of turning his head to one side, like a horse. I would walk around him, like someone circling a statue in a museum. Just as in medieval paintings people hold their heads to one side, so in my memory my father's face is always turned.
>
> There came a time at last when he couldn't look away. He was in a hospital bed and it would have been too painful to turn his head because the illness had spread to his bones. When I placed myself in his line of sight, he had to see me.
>
> It was our last chance to talk and I felt all that I had to say thrilling along my nerves. I had a lifetime of small and large talk saved up. I took a great breath, opened my mouth like an opera singer, but only a sigh came out, because talk doesn't keep. Everything was concreted into lumps, like stuff left too long in the refrigerator. At the very end, I told my father that I would miss him. I did not say that I had always missed him.

My son, who is 15, has a silent face, like a cowboy or a sea captain, like a skier or a flyer. His face is smooth and idealized, like sculpture. It looks air-brushed. If I were to ask him why he doesn't talk to me, he might answer, "About what?"

In his school on the soccer team, my son is taught to accept victory and defeat in silence, with what the Greeks called, *apatheia,* a word rather like our understatement. My son is an athlete of understatement.

Broyard deplores the lack of communication between father and son. But it's really not a new story.

David had great problems of communication with his children. What greater proof of a generation gap is needed than his tragic relationship with his son Absalom, who in David's old age rebelled against him and tried to destroy him.

And something must have gone awry between King Hezekiah, a God-fearing, righteous man, and his son, Menashe, who became one of the most wicked and idolatrous kings in the history of Judea.

And the problem didn't end with the biblical period. There was an interview a while ago in a Hebrew weekly with Assaf Dayan, the son of Moshe Dayan, who had once been Israel's Foreign Minister. Assaf is a movie actor and director, who revealed that when his father was hospitalized for a life-threatening illness some years ago the son learned about it by chance, coming across a story about his father's illness in a newspaper.

Why didn't he know about his father's illness? Because the father and son were almost totally estranged from each other. They used to see each other once a year, on which occasion Moshe Dayan would also see his grandchildren. Assaf's political sympathies were at opposite poles from those of his father. He feels closest to the Rakach Party, which is Communist, and receives virtually all its votes from Israeli Arabs. Clearly, somewhere along the way, the communication broke down between Moshe Dayan and his son.

Are there any insights that we can glean to help us deal with this perennial problem? And does not the same problem exist between mothers and daughters? Is there a way of opening up that elusive process of communication, so that we do not recapitulate this sense of alienation in our own relationships?

In the Passover Haggadah, which we read at our Seder, one of the four sons is described as *"sheeyno yodeya lishol,"*—who doesn't know how to ask the questions, who cannot initiate communication with his father.

What does the Haggadah suggest? *"At p'tach lo."*—You, the father, must open up the channels of communication; otherwise, they may remain closed forever.

If, for some reason, you and your son are angry with each other, and you have stopped talking to each other, and each one waits for the other to take the initiative, you must be the mature one and begin again the indispensable process of communication.

There are too many homes where fathers are not communicating with their sons. A while ago, a colleague of mine invited a psychologist to lead a discussion with a high school class on the problem of communication between parents and children. My colleague sat in the back and listened. As he observed the discussion, he noticed a strange phenomenon: each time a youngster would criticize his parents, he would laugh and the class would laugh with him. A student would recount something terribly painful in his relationship with his parents and he would giggle. The psychologist then asked them about their laughter. They became defensive and said it was the laughter of recognition and then they asserted he wouldn't understand. He then asked them if they were laughing because they were nervous or because they couldn't handle the situation. They vigorously denied that this was the reason. Suddenly, one of the boys in the back of the room turned to my colleague and said quietly. "If you don't laugh, you cry." They were laughing because the subject was so painful that it was their way to keep from crying.

When you have stopped talking to each other, don't stand on ceremony. You be the one to begin so that the relationship can be resumed once again.

But I see yet another meaning in those words of the Haggadah: *"At p'tach lo."* Many men have difficulty in expressing their emotions. We have, after all, been taught from childhood that "a man doesn't cry." But, somehow, we men have to learn how to "open up," to express our feelings to our sons so that they can learn to do the same. Some of us, when we become angry, become quiet and withdrawn. We seethe inside but we cannot express what we are feeling. A boy said to me recently about his parents, "When my mother gets angry, she rants and raves, but when the storm is over, everything is fine. But my father gets very quiet and I know he's very angry. He doesn't say a word but it goes on forever and it's scary!"

We fathers have to learn to express our feelings whether it's anger or grief or love.

In San Diego there is a telephone service for children which is called "Dial a Smile." Carol Baros, a grandmother, has recorded hundreds of inspirational messages for depressed and lonely children. About nineteen thousand children, mostly between the ages of five and ten, call the free twenty-four-hour service each month. The children hear a ninety-second message that is changed each day. One day she will discuss the importance of being kind to parents. Another day she might tell them how they can chase the blues by finding something interesting to do around the house. She explains why the service is so necessary: "Lots of children are very lonely, because almost half of all marriages in California end in divorce and many children don't see as much of both parents as they would like. Frequently grandparents and other relatives live far away and so they aren't available to give the children the love and affection they crave." She receives many fan letters. One ten-year-old wrote: "I called you yesterday and I felt good inside when you told me to go out and smile at our world. I'm going to tell all my friends to dial your number so they will feel better too."

Another ten-year-old girl wrote: "Since I've been listening to your stories every morning, I smile and can always get rid of Mr. Lonesome."

A six-year-old wrote: "My daddy moved away and I miss him. I don't know why he left."

I think this service is a stroke of genius on the part of Carol Baros. But it's also very sad that children have to depend upon a recorded phone message for a little bit of love. The Haggadah says to us, Open up and express your feelings of love for your children, so that they might learn from you how to do the same.

But, the formula of *At p'tach lo* can help us in yet another way. I was interested to read in that interview with Assaf Dayan about his attitude toward Judaism. He dismisses the *mitzvot* of Judaism as "a collection of primitive remnants of the Second Temple period." He sees absolutely no connection between himself and other Jews who are religious. In referring to the *t'filin,* he views the notion that a young boy should get up each morning "and tie himself with straps" as primitive. He sees the belief in God as part of the same primitivism. The interviewer asked him about his own religious upbringing. He said, "My brother and I did not have a Bar Mitzvah. I was in a synagogue only once, as part of an official tour. My parents asked me if I wanted a Bar Mitzvah. I said no—the whole family is atheistic. . . . Our family Seder was very strange. It was a brief ceremony and then we ate. We didn't fast on Yom Kippur and the other holidays had no religious meaning for us. . . ."

No wonder Assaf Dayan has no Jewish identity and feels such antipathy to Judaism. He was never given the opportunity to learn and experience the meaning and beauty of our faith.

What does the Haggadah say? *"At p'tach lo."* If you want your son to be a Jew, then you have to open up for him the world of Jewish Tradition and experience and make it come alive for him. You have to have a real Seder in which both of you take an active part. Encourage him to ask questions, and try to provide the answers. When *Sukkot* comes, build a *sukkah* together and relive the wandering of our people in the wilderness. On *Shabbat*, come to the Synagogue together to pray and learn and to feel yourselves a part of a Jewish community. At mealtime, say a blessing together and talk about something you have studied of the Tradition, and let him, in turn, tell you what he has learned. Unless you "open up the Jewish world to him," it may remain closed all his life.

Do you know who will announce the coming of the Messiah? Our Tradition says that it will be the prophet Elijah. And what will be his first task? The Haftorah of *Shabbat Hagadol* tells us that on that great day, *"V'heyshiv lev avot al banim v'lev banim al avotam"*—He will reconcile fathers with their sons, and sons with their fathers.

If we want to hasten the coming of that great day, we will have to begin the task of reconciliation ourselves and hopefully begin today.

# 17.
# How to Judge People

Was Noah truly a great man for all generations, or was he really a mediocre person who was considered righteous because he lived in the midst of a terrible society? There is a famous debate about this question in the Talmud. The first verse of our *sidrah* says:

> *Noach ish tzadik tamim hayah b'dorotav:*
> "Noah was a righteous man, He was blameless in his generation."

One Rabbi, Resh Lakish, interprets this verse *l'shevach*, as a compliment to Noah. If Noah was able to be righteous in his evil generation, he would have been even greater in a generation of righteous people. But Rabbi Yochanan disagrees. He interprets this verse *lignay*, as discrediting Noah. If Noah had lived in Abraham's generation, nobody would even have noticed him.

I want to respectfully disagree with Rabbi Yochanan and his judgment of Noah. It seems to me that this verse is obviously a compliment to Noah. It says:

> *Noach ish tzadik,*

and to be called a *tzadik* is a great compliment indeed. Furthermore, the verse continues:

> *et haelohim hithalech noach:*
> "Noah walked with God."

Certainly that kind of description bespeaks the greatness of this man.

Why then is the verse interpreted to his discredit? Perhaps Rabbi Yochanan agreed with those students of history who assert that man does not make history but that history makes the man. Noah was outstanding because of his historic situation. Had he lived at another time, he might never have been noticed.

Nevertheless, I believe that Rabbi Yochanan's judgment of Noah represents an altogether too common failing of judging people in a poor light rather than in a favorable one.

Most of us are guilty of this same failing. For example, when we see a successful businessman who has made a fortune, we say, "If I had his *mazal*, I'd be a millionaire too." When we hear about an outstanding student who has achieved a great honor, we say, "He's such a grind, such a bore. If I wanted to spend my whole life with books, I could have done just as well." Or in hearing of the remarkable achievement of a renowned scientist, we say, "Others paved the way and he gets all the credit."

There is a certain amount of truth in each of these assertions. Luck is certainly important to the businessman; a successful student usually does work hard; and a good scientist does not do it all by himself. But that is not the whole truth. Many successful businessmen have had their share of bad breaks; many good students have also found time for athletics and for an interesting social life; and many renowned scientists have been able to see the broader implications of other people's work in order to create genuine breakthroughs in their field.

Why, then, this human proclivity for judging others unfavorably and for refusing to acknowledge their genuine ability? Perhaps it is due to our own insecurity. When we are uncertain of our own role in life, unsure of whether we are succeeding in what we are doing, perplexed about our effectiveness as parents, students, or as people, somebody else's success becomes a great threat to us. When our security is threatened, we find it easier to disparage another rather than face ourselves honestly with our fears and inadequacies. Thus, we say, "They never would have succeeded through their own ability; they had all the breaks."

When we develop more confidence in ourselves and as we learn to measure our own achievements by the honesty of our effort and the integrity of our work instead of constantly comparing ourselves with the achievements of others, we will begin to accept other people and their accomplishments without seeing them as personal affronts to our own egos.

But there is still another way in which we judge others unfavorably. We not only denigrate those who are successful but are also very quick to condemn those who are unsuccessful. About the man who always struggles to make a living, we say, "Once a *shlemihl*, always a *shlemihl*." About a marriage which has ended in failure, we comment, "They were both no angels." About a youngster who has gotten into trouble, we assert, "Maybe if his parents would have spent a little time at home instead of running around constantly, he would have turned out differently."

Again, there is a partial truth to these comments. Some people are *shlemihls, nebich*; some couples are certainly not angelic; and some parents do neglect their children. But really, does anybody need to be reminded that there are many able people who are not terribly successful in their work? Or that there are many fine couples who are simply incompatible? Or that there are many parents who are completely devoted to their children and yet the children sometimes get themselves into serious trouble?

Yet we so often pass judgment so easily, so casually, and so cruelly. We are so ready to find fault, to place the blame, and to cast aspersion.

Why is it that we judge people so unfavorably when they have been unsuccessful? It is, I believe, because we lack the quality of empathy; we lack the ability to put ourselves in another's shoes. How did Hillel, that great teacher and loving human being put it?

> *Al tadin et chavercha ad shetagia limkomo:*
> "Never judge another person until you have stood in his place."

Never judge another until you have lived through his *tsoris*, until you have learned to so identify with him that you can really understand him. Because a person has been unsuccessful, don't be so ready with the damaging label. Perhaps if you had seen how he worked and hoped and struggled and yet could not quite make it, you would feel a little *rachmonus* for him; perhaps you would understand his plight and feel his travail.

If a couple have not been able to "make a go" of their marriage, don't be so ready to condemn them. Perhaps if you knew the great hopes they had when they entered marriage and how they tried to overcome their differences and were not able to do so, if you knew how many outsiders interfered and hurt their marriage instead of helping it, you would feel compassion for them; perhaps you would even feel their heartbreak as their lives are being torn asunder.

Because a youngster has gotten into trouble, don't be so ready to blame his parents. Perhaps if you had seen how much his parents loved him and watched over him and worried about him, if you only knew how much his actions have embarrassed them, hurt them, and shattered them, you would feel compassion for them. Perhaps you would sense their sorrow and their tragedy, and you would say, "There but for the grace of God goes my child."

Only as we learn the precious quality of empathy and begin to identify fully with another person, only then will we stop judging others harshly. Then our condemnation will turn into understanding and our callousness will be transformed into compassion. Only then will we ourselves become fully human.

# 18.
# How We Reveal Ourselves

Each of us constantly reveals more about ourselves than we realize. We may tell another person we are happy but our eyes may tell another story. We may commiserate with another person and say, "I'm sorry," but our face may show indifference. We may speak to another with great confidence but our walk may reveal that we feel defeated.

Our words, our actions, even, some say, our handwriting, reveal more about us than we realize.

One of the fascinating aspects of biblical commentary is not only the varied interpretations of each verse, each adding its own color and richness to the text, but occasionally a comment affords us an intimate revelation into the commentator's soul, revealing more, perhaps, than he himself realized.

Today's Torah reading is a case in point. It depicts God as being angry with Israel for creating and worshiping a golden calf. At one point God threatens Moses with the destruction of the entire people. Moses pleads with Him to forgive the people and in his final plea to God, he cries out in despair: "Forgive their sin, I beg You, and if not . . ."—

> *m'cheyni na misifrecha asher katavta:*
> "Blot me out of Your book which You have written!"

Rashi explains Moses' words with this comment: "Blot me out of Your whole Torah; so that people should not say about me that I was not successful in seeking mercy for my people."

What Moses is saying to God, according to Rashi, is: "If You are willing to forgive Israel, I am willing to continue to lead them. But if You won't forgive them, expunge my name from the record completely because I am a total failure."

Rashi's explanation of the word *"sifrecha,"* Your Book, sees Moses as referring to the Torah.

The Rashbam, Rashi's grandson, who lived in the twelfth century, comments on the words *m'cheyni na misifrecha asher katavta* with the following explanation. Moses says to God: "Wipe me out of Your Book of Life. If my people are going to die, I don't want to live either!"

For the Rashbam, the word *"Sifrecha"* refers to the Book of Life. These are both plausible explanations, very close to the literal meaning of the text.

But there is a very unusual and startling interpretation given by the Ramban, Rabbi Moses ben Nachman, or Nachmanides. He explains Moses' plea to God with these remarkable words:

> *m'cheyni na tachtam miseyfer hachayim va'esbol ani onsham:*
> "Expunge me from Your Book of Life in their stead, and I will suffer their punishment for them!"

As a proof text, he cites a very famous verse from the prophet, Isaiah chapter 53, which says: "But he was wounded because of our transgressions, he was crushed because of our iniquities, and with his stripes we were healed."

Why is that such a remarkable comment? First, because it is very far from the real meaning of the text. And second, because it sounds so much like an important Christian doctrine called Vicarious Atonement, in which Jesus is believed to have died to atone for the sins of humanity. And what is even more remarkable is that the Ramban's proof text from Isaiah 53 is the very text which Christians use in order to show that Isaiah foretold the suffering of Jesus for mankind's sins!

Now if that explanation of Moses' words were given by a Christian scholar, it would make a great deal of sense. But coming from Rabbi Moses ben Nachman, the Ramban, the greatest rabbi of Spain in the thirteenth century, it simply boggles the mind!

In order to understand that comment, it is necessary to take a closer look at the Ramban's life, to see what clues we might find to unravel this mystery.

Moses ben Nachman was born in Gerona, Spain, in 1194. He became a rabbi and a physician. He was one of the greatest scholars of talmudic literature in the Middle Ages. And he was also a philosopher, poet, and biblical commentator. He served as Chief Rabbi of Catalonia for a number of years. Throughout Spain, Jews referred to him as *Harav*, the rabbi, par excellence.

But one of the great traumas in his life came as a result of the missionizing efforts of an apostate Jew, Pablo Christiani. Christiani persuaded King James to invite Nachmanides to Barcelona in 1263 for a public disputation about the merits of Christianity versus Judaism. Christiani's hope was that if he could publicly triumph over the greatest rabbi of Spain, the entire Jewish community would be convinced and would, as a result, convert to Christianity.

Nachmanides reluctantly agreed to take part in the disputation, recognizing the inherent dangers for him and the Jewish community, but one does not refuse an invitation from the king. But he insisted on complete freedom of speech, which the king granted.

The disputation lasted four days. It took place in the king's palace in the presence of the court, distinguished clergy, knights, and ordinary citizens.

Christiani, using legends from the Talmud, tried to prove that the Messiah had already come in the person of Jesus and that he had died to atone for the sins of mankind. Further, with his coming, the commandments of Judaism had lost their validity.

But Nachmanides, by his erudition and scholarship, was able to convince the assemblage that the meaning of the passages had nothing to do with Jesus and Christian teachings. The king, despite his disappointment, felt that Nachmanides had won the debate. He presented Nachmanides with three hundred gold coins and said to him, "I have never seen a man defend a wrong cause so well."

But the Dominicans who had urged the debate could not forgive Nachmanides for winning the disputation. Two years later they hailed him before a royal tribunal and he was charged with blaspheming the Catholic faith. The king, who was a friend of Nachmanides, tried to protect him, but ultimately the pressures became so great and the danger to his life so imminent that at the age of seventy, old, weary, and heartbroken, Nachmanides had to leave his two sons, his community, and all that was familiar and beloved, to flee to *Eretz Yisrael*.

While living in *Eretz Yisrael*, he worked on his Commentary to the Bible and he died there a few years later.

In a brilliant essay, Rabbi Solomon Goldfarb, *alav hashalom*, suggests that this trauma in the Ramban's life is the explanation of his strange comment on the biblical verse. In writing his commentary, when the Ramban approached this account of the confrontation between Moses and God as it was described in the Torah, it was as if he were reliving his own terrible trauma of the dangerous disputation between Pablo Christiani and himself. He therefore has Moses say to God the very words that Christiani said to him about Jesus, namely that Moses is willing to die for Israel's sins. But he does this in order to be able to refute such a belief as non-Jewish, a refutation which comes from God Himself, who says to Moses:

*mi asher chatah li emchenoo misifri:*

Nahmanides interprets these words to mean:

"I will erase from My Book of Life whoever has sinned, but not you, for you have not sinned."

God is saying to Moses: Nobody can give his life to atone for another's sins. Whoever is guilty, that person must stand before Me in judgment.

Thus does Nachmanides reveal, in a comment that is far from the literal meaning of the text, perhaps unconsciously, the pain and tragedy of his disputation and exile from Spain, a trauma whose effects he felt to the end of his days.

We respect the faith of our Christian neighbor and we regard each person's faith as sacred and inviolable. But it is also important for us as Jews to understand ourselves and our own faith particularly in the face of missionizing groups like Jews for Jesus, whose major effort is directed at converting unsuspecting young Jews to Christianity.

Why do we Jews not accept the idea of Vicarious Atonement? First, Judaism sees this doctrine as ethically unjust. We cannot accept the idea of an innocent person dying to save us. Justice requires that the person who sins should bear the consequences of his actions.

And we have another problem with this doctrine. Vicarious Atonement leads to the belief in Jesus as a mediator between humanity and God. But we believe that every human being has equal access to God and that each person can approach God through his prayers, if they are but sincere and honest. Therefore we do not need a mediator between us and God.

Finally, it is our belief that not only can no one atone for our sins nor that we require an intercessor but that it is possible for each person to achieve redemption through *teshuvah*, penitence, which is genuine and wholehearted. Even if a person has sinned grievously, he can atone by making recompense to those against whom he has sinned, and he can achieve forgiveness from God if he genuinely changes his life and lives by the teachings of the Torah.

How did the Prophet Isaiah put it?

> *Yaazov rasha darko v'ish aven machshevotav:*
> "Let the wicked forsake his way
> And the man of iniquity his thoughts";
>
> *v'yashov el hashem virachemyhoo ki yarbeh lisloach:*
> "And let him return unto the Lord,
> And He will have compassion upon him
> And He will abundantly pardon."

Judaism places a great responsibility upon each one of us. It says that if we sin and err, we cannot go through life blaming someone else: our parents, teachers, friends, or society. It is our own fault, our own weakness, and our own insensitivity.

But Judaism says no human being is ever doomed, lost, or hopeless. If we really want to become better people, more compassionate, more concerned, more understanding; if we want to do *teshuvah*, God is waiting for us and will receive us in love just as a loving parent is always ready to accept a child who has become estranged and alienated from him.

When shall we begin this *teshuvah*, this changing of our lives for the better? Rabbi Eliezer addressed himself to that very question when he said to his students, "Repent one day before your death."

But his students objected and said that was impossible, since no one knows the day of his death. Whereupon Rabbi Eliezer responded, "All the more reason to begin today."

# 19.
# Telling the Truth

Without truth, human society and human relationships cannot long endure. A customer has to be able to trust the merchant from whom he makes a purchase. A homeowner has to assume that the tradesperson will do an honest job in repairing his house. A client has to believe his lawyer; a patient has to trust his physician. Unless people tell each other the truth, our most basic relationships must disintegrate.

Therefore, Jewish Tradition places great emphasis upon the importance of truth. In establishing the basic laws and principles which should govern Jewish society, the Torah says, "Keep far from any falsehood." The Talmud puts it even more strongly: "The Holy One, Blessed be He, hates a person who says one thing with his mouth and another in his heart." And after we die, the Talmud says, each one of us will stand in judgment before God and the first question we will be asked is: "Were you honest in your dealings with each person?"

Isn't it strange that this wonderful quality of truth, which our Tradition demands of us, can also become a dangerous weapon? For example, an unfeeling physician may tell his patient, "You have six months to live." I know some patients who were told that and who outlived their doctors.

Or a friend who says to you, "You look terrible!" Till then you felt fine but now, suddenly, you begin to feel ill. I had a great-aunt, an elderly woman with an acerbic tongue, who lived in Williamsburg. When we would visit her, sometimes together with my father who would come in from Pennsylvania to visit me at the Yeshiva, she would invariably greet him with these words, *"Shloime, zehst di ois in drerd!"*—Shlomo, you look horrible! It was the kind of greeting which always made him feel terrible.

Or a person relates a damaging piece of gossip about another.

Someone remonstrates with the speaker and he defends himself by saying, "But I'm telling the truth!" Even if it is true, it is still *rechilut*, calumny, which can destroy another's reputation and is contrary to Jewish Law. I generally find that when somebody begins a conversation with these words "I'm going to be perfectly frank with you," I prepare myself psychologically for the blow which is about to come.

Our tradition shows a profound sensitivity to the danger of truth, and our Rabbis derive this insight from an interesting passage in our *sidrah*. A messenger from God informs Abraham that, in one year, Sarah will give birth to the long-awaited and hoped-for son. But Sarah laughs to herself, saying, "Now that I am withered, am I to have enjoyment and with my husband so old?" God was annoyed with Sarah's reaction and he said to Abraham, "Why did Sarah laugh, saying, 'Shall I in truth bear a child, being so old?' "

The Rabbis noticed an interesting omission by God in reporting Sarah's words to Abraham. She had originally spoken of her elderliness as well as that of Abraham. But when God repeated her comment to Abraham, He mentioned only the fact that she complained of her age, not of Abraham's. Whereupon the Rabbis make this remarkable comment: *"Mutar l'shanot bidvar hashalom she'af hakadosh baruch hu shinah . . . vadoni zaken"*—It is permissible to stretch the truth for the sake of peace, for even God did the same by refraining from mentioning Sarah's words to Abraham. Our Rabbis understand that truth is essential for the good of society, but at times, for the good of society, it may also be necessary to set it aside.

Let me give you some examples of where it is important to stretch the truth. Couples should be truthful to each other. They should be able to fully trust each other, but they don't necessarily have to express every thought that comes to mind because some thoughts may be damaging to the other person. Dr. Karl Scheibe, a psychology professor at Wesleyan University, says, "There is a mischievousness to language. It gives reality to fleeting thoughts, to the doubts and suspicions about others which don't deserve to be made concrete. You cannot say everything that goes through your mind and also maintain a long-term relationship."

In addition to remaining silent on some matters, Dr. Scheibe also prescribes for every marriage what he calls "Elaboration and embroidery of the truth" in order to meet the other's needs. It is important, he maintains, to constantly reassure one another, "I love you. You look wonderful," words which really shouldn't be necessary, but they are. He says that even if those words convey more than what you happen to feel at that moment, they are an expression of faith in the future and make the other person feel good, desirable, and loved.

What we say to children may also require some embroidery of the truth, in order to help them grow into adults with healthy self-images. The psychiatrist Dr. Willard Gaylin points out that children ask parents such questions as "Am I beautiful?" or "Do you love me best of anyone in the world?" He contends that if you tell children the whole truth, it may shape their perception of themselves always. He says, "If you tell a young girl that she's beautiful, she's likely to become a very attractive young woman. If you tell her that she's ugly, even the prettiest girl will believe it and act accordingly. So your answer may determine whether it's true or not."

Our words, then, can help to create the future. That awareness places great responsibility upon us as spouses, parents, and teachers. Perhaps the most awesome responsibility of all is that which is placed upon physicians. What happens when you have to tell a patient that his cancer has spread? Differences of opinion exist among doctors. Some believe that you must tell the patient the unvarnished truth. But other physicians and psychologists are horrified by what they see as heartless "truth-dumping." When you tell a patient, "Your cancer has spread," you may send him into a tailspin and the anxiety can make him even more ill or destroy his will to live, when the situation may actually be far from hopeless.

Dr. Arnold Relman, editor of the *New England Journal of Medicine*, says, "It is difficult for healthy people to understand the terrors of those in life-threatening situations. And the sicker the patients, the more they need reassurance rather than total candor." He says that doctors frequently "dump" the truth to make it easier for themselves rather than for the sake of their patients. Then "they walk away and let the patient handle it," instead of taking responsibility and facing the pain together with the patient. He believes that the best prescription is a gradual, more gentle approach to the truth. According to him, "direct questions should be answered honestly and clearly. Unrequested information should be offered only when the doctor believes it is necessary for the patient."

At times, it may be necessary for each of us to "embroider" the truth.

Well, then, how do you determine the difference, when absolute truth is required and when "stretching" the truth is necessary?

Judaism says the truth should always be the base from which we operate; a person's word must be sacred in his work and in his relationships with others. But if we believe that the truth will hurt another person, we don't necessarily have to say it.

A Yiddish proverb teaches: *A ligend tor men nit zogen ober dem emes darf men nit zogen*—You must not tell a lie, but you don't have to give expression to every truth that comes to mind. In addition, if "embroidering" the truth can enhance or encourage another person, then you may do so, whether it is to a spouse, a child, a student, or a patient.

There is a wonderful discussion in the Talmud between the School of Shammai and the School of Hillel about what you should say to a bride at her wedding. It is a *mitzvah* to sing, dance, and entertain the bride and groom. But the Rabbis ask the question: *"Keytzad m'rakdim lifney hakalah?"*—How do you describe the bride as you dance before her? *Bet* Shammai, who were literalists, said, "Describe her as she is." If she's not beautiful, don't exaggerate. But *Bet* Hillel differed with them and said you should say, *"Kallah naah vachasudah"*—the bride is beautiful and graceful. *Bet* Shammai protested and pointed out, "After all, the Torah teaches: *"Midvar sheker tirchak"*—keep away from falsehood! But *Bet* Hillel understood a greater truth, which is that every bride is beautiful and your words can make her feel even more beautiful, even if you have to "embroider" the truth a little bit.

Our Tradition says that *emet*, truth, is the seal of God, His own signature. Sometimes when we "embroider" the truth, it is our way of emulating God's qualities of love and compassion for all His children.

# 20.
# When People Count

Most of us find statistics very boring. Yet in the first chapter of *Bamidbar*, all we are given are a series of numbers as God tells Moses to take a census of the people of Israel.

As you read this chapter, a number of questions arise. First, since the Torah is a book which contains all kinds of edifying and ethical teachings, one wonders what we can possibly learn from all of these statistics? And why the need for yet another census? There was, after all, a previous census taken before the building of the *Mishkan*, the Tabernacle.

Moses Nachmanides, who lived in Spain during the thirteenth century, suggests the following reason for a second census: "After every plague, God numbers Israel to make known that though He wounds, His hands make whole again . . ."

After the first census, Israel had sinned by worshiping the Golden Calf. A great plague followed and many Israelites died. Therefore God ordered Moses to take another census in order to comfort the Israelites by showing them that despite the plague and despite their losses, the nation still consisted of a great many people—603,550, to be exact.

It is one of the anomalies of Jewish history that the more we were persecuted, the more we prospered. When the Israelites were in Egyptian bondage, Pharaoh tried to destroy them but the Torah tells us:

> *Kaasher y'anoo oto keyn yirbeh v'yifrotz:*
> "The more they afflicted them, the more they multiplied and spread out."

Our people were persecuted during the Middle Ages, economically, politically, and socially. Our enemies restricted our opportunities for making a livelihood. We were herded into ghettos and forced to wear a badge of shame. Despite it all, our people lived on, multiplied in numbers, and increased its intellectual and ethical achievements.

When Hitler took power, he destroyed six million of us, and yet, today, we Jews have our own state once again. With all of its problems, it is nonetheless alive, vital, and full of energy. If Hitler were able to view that state, he would turn over in his grave.

Under Andropov, Russian Jews suffer discrimination, persecution, and imprisonment, and yet they refuse to give up and they refuse to die. Instead, they demand the right to emigrate and to be Jews.

A few years ago, a New York stockbroker, Morton Leventhal, was visiting Israel. Armed only with an electric mine detector and a Boy Scout knife, he stumbled upon one of the rarest and most valuable archeological treasures. In an agricultural field near Bet Shaan, overlooking the Jordan River, he found a life-size, magnificently carved bronze statue of Emperor Hadrian, dating from the second century. He took the statue to his sister's *kibbutz*, Tirat Tzvi, where it was placed in the dining hall. The field in which the statue was found adjoins Tel Shalem, which is believed to be the site of one of the fortified Roman settlements built along the Jordan. Hadrian's sixth Roman legion was in that area and the soldiers may have had the statue cast in his honor.

The statue is a very rare discovery. There is only one other life-size bronze of Hadrian in the Archeological Museum in Istanbul. It is ironic that the statue should have resurfaced in Israel, since Hadrian was a notoriously cruel ruler of ancient Judea who crushed the Bar Kochba revolt in 135 C.E. and enslaved and persecuted thousands of Jews.

Dr. Cornelius Vermeule, curator of Greek and Roman art at Boston's Museum of Fine Arts, made a most incisive comment about this remarkable discovery. He characterized the find as a "mighty symbol of Jewish survival after two millennia" and went on to say: "Hadrian might have sought to bury the Jewish people, but clearly it is the Roman Emperor, released from earth's captivity, who was bidden to breakfast at a *kibbutz*."

Why did God tell Moses to conduct a second census? To remind the people of Israel that despite the plagues and persecutions directed against them, their enemies had ultimately perished but they were still alive and flourishing as a people.

## Living Courageously

Nachmanides saw yet another important reason for this census. It is significant, he points out, that in the instruction for counting the people, the words used are:

> *kol zachar l'gulgelotam:*
> "Count each man, individually."

To which Nachmanides comments: when you count the total number of your people, be very sure that you never forget the individual: his importance, dignity, and needs.

Ours is an age when we need this reminder very much.

In totalitarian countries like Russia and China, as they create their "utopias," thousands may die in the process, deaths which are unimportant to their governments, for, they feel, those who die will simply be replaced by others.

In our society many have become Organization Men, where each person must help strengthen the corporate image. Even a man's wife is screened to find out if she fits the image. He must refashion himself in accordance with the needs of his giant employer despite the danger of the loss of his own individuality.

Our children, from the moment they enter school, are encouraged to conform, to comply, and to submerge their own personalities, for the consideration of what is sometimes called by educators "classroom management."

I was recently shown the report card of a kindergartner, whom I know to be a bright, intelligent, and inquiring five-year-old. On it, the teacher wrote: "He is not as much of a problem as he used to be. He now is learning to conform. He is much quieter. I am very pleased." What she is really saying is that this little boy, full of intellectual curiosity and *joie de vivre*, has been sufficiently cowed by her constant disapproval to hide his real feelings and is now much easier for her to manage.

It is important to remember that individuals who are not stifled and who are permitted to give free reign to their creativity can sometimes accomplish miracles.

In Israel there is a man named Yaakov Maimon, who admits to being over seventy. He is the author of the Maimon Method, the most widely used system of Hebrew shorthand, and he still does the shorthand recordings of the weekly meetings of the Israeli Cabinet. But for the most part, Yaakov is involved in a project of his own creation: the activation of thousands of people in becoming volunteers to teach new immigrants the Hebrew language or any other subject they want to know. His method is simple. He is told by the authorities where the latest group of immigrants are being settled. In a short time, Yaakov is there, going from apartment to apartment, asking, "Is there anyone here who would like help with his studies?" The offer applies to everybody: men, women, and children. Then he mobilizes his volunteers, mostly high school youngsters and members of women's organizations. They come to the immigrants' homes and give them lessons, helping them become integrated into Israeli society.

He operates everywhere: Jerusalem, Haifa, Ashdod. He gets weekly reports from the volunteer teachers, keeps records, encourages everybody who is involved. He works on a shoestring budget of six thousand dollars a year, made up of contributions, money which is mostly spent on trucks that bring the volunteers to the new settlement areas. Yaakov Maimon is a one-man educational institution, an individual with an *idée fixe*, who is helping to educate thousands of people.

When you count people, the Torah tells us, never forget the infinite potentialities that exist in each individual.

And finally, Nachmanides discerns one more great teaching in this census of our people. God tells Moses to count people who are

*yotzey tzavah:*
"Count each person who is able to do battle."

In a time of battle, the verse suggests, each person must be prepared to stand up and be counted and each age has its own battles.

In the Bible, Israel prepared to do battle for the Promised Land.

In our day, we still need people who are willing to do battle against those who would keep others from achieving their Promised Land. We need to do battle against dictators like Assad and Kadaffi who would deprive Israel of its homeland. We need to help those who fight against a despot like Andropov who would deprive our people of their birthright. We need to fight against the anti-Semites who are always ready to defame and destroy our people.

One of the first Jews who came to this country from Brazil was a man named Asser Levy, who originally stemmed from Amsterdam. Levy was a great battler for the rights of Jews to be equal citizens with their neighbors. He objected to the discriminatory tax that was levied upon Jews as a compulsory substitute for military service, which was expected of all other people. He petitioned for the right to stand guard in defense of New Amsterdam. When that right was refused, he simply proceeded to perform his military duties anyway until the authorities finally agreed to permit him to do so officially. Some months later, he presented a second petition to the effect that since he had now participated in military duties with other burghers, he asked to become a full burgher, which he had been in Amsterdam. Again, the court denied his request but he appealed over its head to the Director General and Council of the colony, and he won.

It was because of the willingness of Asser Levy to do battle for his rights that the Jews of New York were granted equal rights as citizens, a battle from which each American Jew has been a beneficiary.

The verse says:

*kol yotzey tzavah:*
"There are times when each person must be prepared to stand up and be counted!"

# 21.
# Requisites of the Good Life

Each day brings with it new dilemmas, more uncertainties, and added complexities to our lives. Each one of us is constantly seeking for answers, for ways to deal with life and the problems that it brings our way. Our tendency is to seek wisdom in each new book; guidance in each new psychological theory; help in each opinion expressed by a current authority. Often we lose sight of the fact that these problems did not begin with us and we forget that wisdom did not begin either with us or with our contemporaries.

There are ancient books that contain the experiences and insights of great human beings who faced similar problems and who have attempted to give their solutions and answers to life's perennial questions.

One of the most beautiful and profound books of wisdom is found in the Talmud. It is called *Pirkay Avot*, The Ethics of the Fathers. In this little volume there are contained the teachings of some sixty Rabbis who lived and taught over a period of nearly five hundred years. I would like to share with you the teaching of one of these Rabbis, Yehoshua ben Perachya, who lived in the second century B.C.E. This teaching reflects his attempt to provide a coherent pattern of life in order to give meaning to human existence.

First, Rabbi Yehoshua said:

*Ahsay lecha rav:*
"Provide a teacher for yourself."

Judaism, says Rabbi Yehoshua, places great emphasis upon education. By education, he means not only a course of study to be used as a means to earn a living, however important that may be, but a real education which stimulates us to a constant study of literature, art, poetry, and music. To be educated means to want to benefit from the treasures of civilization, the gifts of the mind and heart created by countless generations which add so much beauty and meaning to life.

Of course, Rabbi Yehoshua was not only interested in our acquainting ourselves with the insights of world civilization. *Ahsay lecha rav* meant preeminently the importance of the study of Torah for every Jew. There are still so many Jews in our day who are brilliant scholars in their own specialties, in science, law, medicine, and other fields, but who possess only an infantile understanding of their own Tradition. They judge their Tradition on the basis of some of their immature, childhood recollections. Therefore, Rabbi Yehoshua says, "Ahsay lecha rav," regardless of your age, regardless of your background, regardless of whether you went to a Hebrew School or not, it is never too late to acquire a teacher, to begin the study of our great Tradition and our great Jewish civilization. No Jew should remain with an infantilized understanding of his great Tradition.

I would suggest to you that Rabbi Yehoshua had another meaning in mind as well when he said, *"Ahsay lecha rav."* Perhaps what he also meant was that everybody needs a Rebbe! The Hasidim, you know, have their Rebbe, who is their guide and model and to whom they turn whenever they need counsel of any kind. But even for those of us who are not Hasidim, I would suggest that we also need a Rebbe. We also need a model who serves as an exemplar of what we would like to become as human beings.

To some, the model is a parent whom we love; for others it is an inspired teacher; for some it is a devoted friend. But what each one of us needs is somebody who will believe in us, who will recognize our potential, who will elicit from us the best of which we are capable.

For many years, there was a senior editor of the Viking Press whose name was Pascal Covicci. He was not well known outside the book publishing industry but to the many writers whom he helped, he was very special. He had a gift for getting writers to do their best work. He did not just edit their writings; he became involved with their personal problems and they received from him comfort, encouragement, and strength. One of his most famous writers was John Steinbeck, who would often begin his day by writing a letter to Mr. Covicci and then carry the theme of his letter into his work. John Steinbeck once said about this man: "Only a writer can understand how a great editor is father, mother, teacher, personal devil and personal God. For nearly forty years, Pat was my collaborator, my conscience. He demanded of me more than I had and thereby caused me to be more than I should have been without him."

*Ahsay lecha rav* means that everybody needs a guide, a mentor, an ideal, if he is to fulfill his own greatest potential.

Rabbi Yehoshua went on to say that there is a second requisite for creating a good and meaningful life:

*K'nay lecha chaver:*
"Acquire a friend."

There is a Yiddish proverb which says: "Friends are needed both for joy and for sorrow." Each one of us in life needs a friend with whom we can share our deepest feelings and hopes, our dreams and disappointments. It is only a friend, a genuine friend, who can truly rejoice with us when we succeed, and it is only a friend who can truly sympathize with us when we fail. When we are successful, there are many people who surround us and who adulate us. When we fail, however, we are left very much alone, to bear our burdens in lonely isolation. That is why somebody once said that a real friend is one who walks in when the rest of the world walks out.

When we are adolescents, perhaps more than at any other time in our lives, friends become the most important people in the world for us. At that age, we barely tolerate our parents. Our brothers and sisters become unnecessary nuisances. But our friends become our confidantes, our guides, our mentors. We are particularly concerned in those years about the opinions of our friends and peers. We would rather die than be different from the group, and it is our peers and friends who determine how we shall dress, talk, and wear our hair. Their pressure is ever-present and unending. All the more reason why Rabbi Yehoshua would say to those of us who are in our teen years: *"K'nay lecha chaver."* "Acquire a friend" has a special meaning. It says, choose your friends very wisely and carefully because there are some friends who can mislead you very badly. There are some people and some friends who are seeking thrills and excitement; who are anxious to experiment with anything that seems dangerous and forbidden, whether it be stealing cupcakes from a Supermarket or trying a new drug that can produce a better high! Often young people get into very serious trouble not because they are inherently bad but because they find it impossible to resist the pressure of those about them, who tell them, "If you don't do what we are doing, you are not going to be a part of this group!"

Rabbi Yehoshua says: *"K'nay lecha chaver":* acquire a friend, by all means, but make sure that your friend is a *Mentch;* make sure that he or she is the kind of human being with whom you can share the values that are important and precious to you.

Rabbi Yehoshua had a third and final teaching. In his attempt to help us create the pattern of a good life, he taught:

*vehevay dan et kol ha'adam l'kaf zchut:*
"Judge each person in the scale of merit."

Rabbi Yehoshua was very well aware that each of us is constantly judging the other, and some people have a special proclivity for finding fault with others. If they are in the classroom, they are the kind of people who make fun of their classmates who are not as bright or who may be a little clumsy and who are not doing exactly the same as the other students.

But it is not limited to the classroom. There are some people who delight in spreading rumors about other people. "Aha!" they say, "did you hear that story?" There are some people who love to share a bit of gossip about another person; and for some, to learn a new tidbit about another is enough to make an evening a great success.

Aside from the fact that judging people in this way hurts them and harms their reputation, Rabbi Yehoshua would affirm that it does strange things to us as well. When you develop this kind of attitude of always judging people negatively, you will find that you will ultimately develop a personality which is suspicious and fearful of everybody. Every person becomes a potential enemy waiting for an opportunity to harm you. Rabbi Yehoshua says that it is a terrible way for a human being to live.

He knew that there are some people in the world who are dangerous and that you have to be very careful in dealing with such people. But what he was saying to each of us was that in the ordinary dealings with ordinary human beings like most of us, it is worth trying another method of judging people. Judge them, he said, *"l'kaf zchut"*: try to give a person the benefit of the doubt. Regardless of what others are saying, try to be the kind of person who finds some redeeming feature in another person. And if you look hard enough, you will usually find that there is a *zchut*, that everybody has some part of his or her life that is good and redeeming. Try to be the kind of person who concentrates on those kinds of attributes rather than on the others.

If you look at the words of Rabbi Yehoshua very carefully, you will discover that the Hebrew has a very important additional meaning. He does not say, *"hevay dan kol adam"*—Judge every man. He says, *"Hevay dan et kol* haadam." The definite article in the Hebrew adds this meaning to his words: Judge the *entire* person in the scale of merit. If you really get to know the whole person, if you really understand another person's problems and tragedies, you will certainly judge him far more charitably and with far greater compassion.

Longfellow once said, "Believe me, every man has his secret sorrows which the world knows not. Oftentimes we call a man cold when he is only sad."

When next you judge a person, says Rabbi Yehoshua, judge him in the scale of merit. Not only will you be a source of far greater help and comfort to the person whom you are judging, but to your own surprise, you will find yourself becoming a more accepting, open, and loving human being in all of your relationships with other people.

# 22.
# The Letters of *Breshit*

On *Sukkot* our Temple was given a precious gift, a Torah which was written in the city of Vilna in Lithuania, a city called by Jews *"Yerushalayim d'lita"*—Jerusalem of Lithuania.

In the eighteenth century a great Rabbi, Elijah ben Solomon, the Gaon of Vilna, wrote a commentary on the Bible. In it he attempted to show that every word of the Bible is necessary and that not even one letter is superfluous.

Take a look, for example, at the first word of today's *sidrah*, the first word of the Torah: *Breshit*. The Gaon said that each letter of that word has a special meaning, and when you put them all together they provide a wonderful pattern of life.

The *bet* stands for *bitachon*, faith. A person must have *bitachon*, for without it life becomes unbearable. *Bitachon* means to believe in God, not only in good times, but even when life becomes very difficult, in the face of defeat or loss. To give up belief in God is to question whether life has any meaning or whether life is simply a cruel hoax. To believe in God is to insist that life is good and that one can make something worthwhile of one's life regardless of every setback.

On the wall of a cellar in Cologne, where a number of escaped prisoners hid from the Nazis during the war, there was found this inscription:

> I believe in the sun, even when it is not shining.
> I believe in love, even when feeling it not.
> I believe in God, even when He is silent.

*Bitachon* means to believe in God even when it is most difficult to do so.

The second letter of *breshit* is *resh*, and this letter, according to the Gaon, symbolizes another basic requisite of human life, which is *ratzon*, will. Some people are always finding excuses for themselves. They say, "I'm messed up because of my parents, they ruined my life," or they complain, "My teachers are terrible, that's why I can't learn a thing," or they maintain, "Life has given me a rotten deal." The implication is: "I'm stuck. I can't do a thing about my life. Circumstances have conspired to destroy me."

*Resh* stands for *ratzon*, will.

Of course, our parents, our teachers, and our environment all have had a profound impact upon us, but each of us still has our own will, and we can change our own lives.

Who had a better excuse for giving up on life than the late folksinger and composer Woody Guthrie. His father's business in Omaha went bankrupt. Two of the family's houses were destroyed by fire, a third by a cyclone. His sister Clara was killed in an oil stove explosion. His mother died of Huntington's Chorea, the same disease that ultimately destroyed Woody as well. And yet, with all his difficulties, he wrote more than a thousand songs that echoed the glory and travail of American life. He always sang of the beauty of America. Perhaps his best known song is "This Land Is Your Land." He also sang songs protesting the sham and injustice of American life.

He once expressed his philosophy this way:

> I hate a song that makes you think that you're not any good. I hate a song that makes you think that you are born to lose. Bound to lose. No good to nobody. No good for nothing. Because you are either too old or too young or too fat or too slim or too ugly or too this or too that. Songs that run you down or songs that poke fun at you on account of your bad luck or your hard traveling. I am out to fight those kinds of songs to my very last breath of air and my last drop of blood.

Woody Guthrie had *ratzon*, the will to make something good and creative of his life, and therefore he did.

The next letter of *breshit* is *aleph*, and that, said the Gaon, stands for *ahavah*, love. To be able to love another person is another requisite of a fulfilled life.

Dostoevski once wrote:

> Fathers and teachers,
> I ponder "What is hell?"
> I maintain that it is the suffering of being unable to love.

What happens to us when we cannot love? If I cannot love another, I cannot transcend myself and go beyond my own petty concerns. The only thing that is important in life is what happens to me, and therefore, each minor hurt becomes a major tragedy. My needs, my health, my worries, all become my obsession. I have no way of ever forgetting my needs as I become absorbed in the needs of another.

Let me tell you about a man by the name of Herman Krausner who lives on New York's Lower East Side. For many years he worked with his brother in a linen supply business. Every night, after work, he would visit strangers who were patients at the V.A. hospital or Maimonides or Bellevue. Four years ago the business was sold, and a year later Herman's brother Jacob died. Then Herman Krausner, at age sixty-nine, began to go blind, and he could no longer make his hospital visits. Instead, he makes about fifteen telephone calls every day to shut-ins, people who are elderly or handicapped, who can't leave their homes, and who warm to the voice of a stranger they have never seen. He often calls blind people, talks to them, cheers them up, finds out how they are managing. Once he was even able to save a woman from committing suicide by his calls.

When asked why he made all those visits in the past and now these telephone calls, he answered; "I just love people. I get a bigger kick from visiting hospitals than I do from going to a show."

Mrs. Eva Garcia, director of the Division of Volunteer Services, said about him, ". . . now that he's blind, it hasn't caused any depression. His attitude is, 'I'm handicapped, but that doesn't mean I should hide my head in the sand—I should do more.' "

Herman Krausner cannot be defeated because he personifies *ahavah*, love of others.

The fourth letter of *breshit* is *shin*. *Shin* stands for *shtikah*, silence. Silence seems like a strange quality to cultivate, but a wise lady explained the need of silence to me recently when she said, "As your children go through the difficult years of adolescence, you learn, as a parent, to be silent very often, otherwise you get your head chewed off. When your children get married, it is even more important to learn how to be silent. They have to make their own mistakes and heaven help you if you try to prevent them!"

How did *Kohelet* put it? "*Et lachashot v'et l'daber*"—There is a time to speak and a time to be *silent*.

The next letter is *yud*, which symbolizes *yirah*, reverence. The Code of Jewish Law begins with these words of the Psalmist:

*Shiviti Hashem L'Negdi Tamid:*
"I am aware of Your Presence, O Lord, at all times."

Judaism teaches that everything a person does in life should reflect his reverence for God. He should use words for healing and not for hurting. He should take actions for sustaining and not destroying. Even the food he eats should not simply satisfy a biological need but should make possible a divine encounter at each meal.

Finally, the last letter, *tav*, stands for Torah. Each Jew has been given a blueprint of life through the Torah. It teaches us how to live with each other and with God. It teaches us to do justice and to love mercy. It teaches us how to live a life of goodness, of compassion, of holiness. It teaches us how to become fully human and, hopefully, a little less than divine.

Thus you have the word *breshit* with the interpretation of the Gaon of Vilna:

*Bitachon*—Faith
*Ratzon*—Will
*Ahavah*—Love
*Shtikah*—Silence
*Yirah*—Reverence
*Torah*—The source of all of these qualities

# 23.
# Why We Should Not Eat of the Tree of Knowledge

One of the fascinating mysteries of the Creation story is why God does not want Adam and Eve to eat of the Tree of Knowledge. Every Bible scholar has tried his hand at answering that question. The words of the Torah are so cryptic and mysterious: *Umeyetz hadaat tov vara lo tochal mimenoo.* God says: "You shall not eat of the Tree of good and evil . . ."

What is the meaning of *tov vara*—good and evil? One scholar says it is a euphemism for sexual passion. The difficulty with that interpretation is that in Judaism, when a couple is married, the sexual relationship is considered holy, then why shouldn't Adam and Eve know about it?

Another scholar suggests that *tov vara* refers to the ability to discern right from wrong. This interpretation raises the question: did God want Adam and Eve to remain amoral? Isn't the essence of the Torah's purpose to teach people how to live moral lives?

I like the interpretation of a third scholar, John Skinner. He writes: "Man's primitive state was one of childlike innocence and purity; and the knowledge he obtained (from the Tree of Knowledge) was the knowledge of life and of the world, which distinguished the grown man from the child." In other words, Skinner maintains that the reason God forbade Adam and Eve from eating of the Tree of Knowledge was in order to prevent them from losing their childlike innocence and purity too quickly and from suddenly acquiring the kind of knowledge that would transform them into adults.

What's wrong with that, you say? Imagine eating a fruit and saving yourself a fortune in college tuition.

By prohibiting Adam and Eve from eating of the Tree of Knowledge, God wanted to teach them and us a number of lessons about life and the process of growing up. First, children cannot be given knowledge of life from external sources. As parents, we are always trying to shield our children from making mistakes. We say to them, "Don't go to that school" or "Don't go into that kind of work" or "Don't marry that person" or "Don't take that risk." Parents are so well meaning but it really doesn't work. A child must make his own mistakes, endure his own suffering, and learn from his own experience. No Tree of Knowledge can be a substitute for experience.

God intended another lesson by prohibiting the fruit of that Tree of Knowledge. If at all possible, a child should not be exposed to life's tragedies too early in life. The problem of divorce has now become widespread in our society. Some couples are truly incompatible and should be divorced. Some, perhaps, could have stayed together if they would have tried harder—but then who can really judge another couple? But one thing is clear: the children of divorce suffer a great deal. They see scenes that children should not see. They hear words that children should not hear. They are torn in their conflicting loyalties to both parents.

A while ago, I was talking to a young boy in my study before his Bar Mitzvah, whose parents had been divorced. We talked about school, his hobbies, his Bar Mitzvah that was coming up. When we concluded our conversation, I rose to say good-bye. Instead of getting up, he put his head on my desk and began to cry. I asked, "Did I say something to hurt you?" He replied, "No, I just want to stay with you a little more." I told him to stay and to come in to see me regularly, which he did. The pain which that boy has felt has already deprived him of a part of his childhood.

There was one more lesson God had in mind in prohibiting the eating from that Tree of Knowledge. Children should not be filled with cynicism too early in life. It's the kind of cynicism which comes from hearing a conversation in which a parent gloats at having put one over on a customer or a competitor. It comes from teaching children never to trust anybody. It develops from constantly reminding children that people want to harm them.

Admittedly, this presents a real dilemma for parents. We don't want our children to become cynics, but at the same time we don't want them to be total innocents either. A child needs a little fear because he or she has to know that there are insane people in the world who put rat poison into fruit on Halloween. They have to know that there is the possibility of tragedy in life, like illness or death; otherwise, you don't prepare them for life. As parents, we always walk a fine line between preserving innocence and inculcating cynicism, but the lesson of the Tree of Knowledge is to emphasize the greater need in childhood of preserving the qualities of innocence and purity.

How does the rest of that mysterious verse continue? It says: *Ki b'yom acholcha mimenoo mot tamut.* God says to Adam and Eve: "On the day you eat of that tree, you will die." But Adam and Eve ate of the Tree and they didn't die until many years later.

Perhaps what God meant was that if you partake too soon of the knowledge of life and the world, something precious and irreplaceable within you will die, the quality of childlike innocence and purity. The great psychologist Erik Erikson once put it: "The most deadly of all sins is the mutilation of a child's spirit."

Why is it so important for children to retain their innocence and purity? It is those very qualities which are an integral part of childhood, which they need to help them enjoy life fully at each stage of their life. In childhood, children should be able to play, to make friends, to explore, daydream, imagine, and fantasize. They should not be burdened by worries, fears, and cynicism, which will come later on. If "the child is father of the man," as the poet put it, if children enjoy their childhood, hopefully they will carry that same enjoyment of life into each stage of their growth, and as adults they will be able to alternately work and play, struggle and relax, produce and enjoy. Children need to retain childhood qualities in order to grow into healthy adulthood.

Children need the qualities of innocence and purity, not only to enjoy childhood and adulthood but to develop a feeling of security and trust in life. They have to feel that their parents love them more than anybody else in the world and that they will take care of them and protect them. With that kind of feeling, children can grow up facing life with confidence instead of fear. According to Erikson, this feeling begins in the first year of life and it represents the first stage in the human life cycle. He calls it "Trust vs. Mistrust." He says that if an infant's needs are met as they arise, if he is cuddled, fondled, played with, and talked to, he develops a sense of the world as a safe place and of people as helpful and dependable. But if the care is inconsistent, inadequate, and rejecting, it fosters a basic mistrust in the child, an attitude of fear and suspicion on the part of the infant toward the world and toward people. Children need innocence, purity, and love to develop a feeling of trust in life.

There is one more reason why children need qualities of innocence and purity. They need always to preserve those childlike qualities to prevent them from becoming old. Some people may age but somehow they never really get old. They always retain an innocence, an enthusiasm, an openness to life and to people, like the scientist who never ceases to be curious about nature and life, or the person who eagerly looks forward to a gathering where she is likely to meet new people, or people who enjoy traveling and who are excited about seeing new places and sharing new experiences.

In New York City there is a group called the New York Enthusiasts, which thrives on new experiences. Its members are not interested in ordinary sightseeing, like the Statue of Liberty or Grant's Tomb. They love the unusual, like a visit to a Buddhist Temple, or spending an hour or two with a prominent painter or writer, or going behind the scenes of a theater, restaurant, or bank, or accompanying an ornithologist on a stroll through a park.

The group's founder is Hans Hacker, who came to this country from Vienna as a refugee in 1938, when he began a love affair with New York. He is seventy years old, suffers from crippling arthritis, and has to use crutches to get around. He arranges about a dozen adventures each month for his group. The group consists of 130 members who range in age from the thirties to the seventies. The members are lawyers, physicians, businessmen, teachers, and secretaries. It includes some couples who first met on an outing of the Enthusiasts.

Such people will never become old. They retain an innocence, openness, and enthusiasm for life which will make them childlike and youthful always.

Erik Erikson once summed it up by saying: "Man is born only with the capacity to learn to hope . . ." Our task is to so nurture a child that the hopes and dreams of childhood will never disappear but will be transformed into adult aspirations and goals that will seek always to strengthen, enjoy, and enhance the quality of human life.

# 24.
# Making a Will

In my Sisterhood Bible course, our last session is a *siyum*. During that session the students ask me questions which they have accumulated on any subject of interest, even if they are not necessarily related to Bible. This year a student told us about a problem which we found to be so thought-provoking that I want to share it with you, together with our reactions to the problem.

The problem had developed with a family living in another community, and the resulting bitterness had torn the family apart. The parents in this family had two children, a son and a daughter. The father lived on for many years after his wife's death and he was ill for many years. His daughter would visit him every day, doing the necessary shopping and chores. She was always a completely devoted and loving daughter.

The son, though living nearby, seldom visited his father. He would call occasionally but generally showed no great interest in him. When the father died, his will was read. Somewhere along the way, he had changed it, leaving the bulk of his large estate to his daughter and a minuscule sum to his son. The son was outraged and he contested the will in court but lost. As a result, the brother and sister stopped speaking to each other for many years.

Recently, the brother called his sister and told her he had just become a grandfather. He apologized for the words he had used to her and the actions he had taken against her. He pleaded with her to restore their broken relationship. The sister has agreed to try to reestablish their relationship but she commented to her friend, "I found I could forgive, but I can't forget."

Who is to blame for the destruction of this family? First, the father is at fault. He proved the truth of the dictum: If you want to destroy your family, leave a will with unequal bequests to your children. Such a will creates fierce antagonism between brothers and sisters. It reawakens old sibling rivalries that go back to earliest childhood. The father bears the primary responsibility.

The daughter, too, can be faulted for not sharing the will equally, despite what her father had done. Logically, she obviously deserved to receive more of the estate. She was always there when her father needed her. But emotions are not necessarily logical, and unless you are willing to share equally with a brother or sister you will create a reservoir of resentment and anger which can inundate the entire family.

How about the brother? Does he share in the blame for taking his sister to court? Unquestionably. People should try to work out their problems privately within the family. To go to court against a member of the family, like writing an unequal will, is another certain way to destroy a family.

In this family there is plenty of blame to go around; all share in the disintegration of their *mishpacha*. Perhaps each of the members of the family suffered from a serious distortion of values: money was more important to them than their family. The father, accustomed to using money to reward and punish, wanted to wield his authority over his family even after death, even if it meant tearing the family apart in the process. The daughter, angry with her brother for his lack of interest in their father, was willing to accept most of the money even though she must have realized the harmful consequences to her family. The son, in his resentment over losing money, was willing to use an outside force to impose his will upon his sister, even if the family would disintegrate in the process. All of them helped to destroy their own family because money was more important to them than love.

Can you forget such a hurt when it happens in your own family? Probably not, but you don't have to dwell on it. I was talking to a couple recently and in the course of the conversation, the husband said, "My wife has a perfect memory. She never lets me forget anything I've ever done."

That kind of memory is not such an admirable trait. We need good memories in order to be able to function at home, at work, and at play. But a "perfect memory" is very bad. Remembering every hurt that has come our way—every insult, argument, mistake—places an intolerable burden on ourselves and on the other person. Every argument, instead of being put into its proper perspective, carries with it the crushing weight of the entire past and can transform an ordinary skirmish into an all-out war.

The French writer Balzac put it very succinctly when he said, "Life cannot go on without much forgetting."

Can this woman ever forget the hurt done her by her brother? Probably not, but she doesn't have to focus on it for the rest of her life. Each of us needs to cultivate the art of "selective remembering." We have to try to remember and savor the good things that happen to us in life: the *simchas*, the moments of happiness, the worthwhile accomplishments. We have to try to remember the good qualities of people: the kindness, the sharing, the help they give us.

We have to try to forget the harmful and sad things in life: the defeats, frustrations, and failures. We have to try to forget the selfishness, pettiness, and rancor.

Will it always work? No, not perfectly. We may not forget all of our negative experiences, but it's worth trying because it can make our lives far more pleasant and more livable.

Is it ever possible to forgive a terrible hurt like the one suffered by this sister? Yes, because otherwise there is no possibility of sustaining human relationships. We all hurt each other; we hurt even those we love most: brothers and sisters, parents and children, husbands and wives. All of us hurt each other even in our most intimate relationships. If we can never forgive each other, we will cut ourselves off from those who are most precious to us.

That is the reason God gave us the gift of *Yom Kippur*. If we are sincere in asking Him for forgiveness, then *Yom Kippur* assures us that God will forgive us, and pardon us, and accept us once again. And if we want God to forgive us, we have to be willing to forgive His children as well.

This father left most of his money to his daughter after his death. The question we should ask ourselves is, when should we give our money away? I believe we should do it while we are still alive. We should give it to our children, intelligently and carefully, and watch them enjoy what we have given to them.

I officiated at the funeral of a father who used to send his adult children on trips because he enjoyed being able to give them these exciting experiences.

Recently, a woman in our congregation took her grandchildren to Israel. She wanted to be there to see the joy of their discovering *Eretz Yisrael*.

But I don't think we have to give everything to our children. They will manage through their own work and ability. We have to give to the great causes that need our help, like our own Temple, the

Jewish Theological Seminary, the Solomon Schechter Day School, and the Combined Jewish Philanthropies.

I heard about a man who came to a meeting recently. At that meeting he learned that some students would not be able to become rabbis because they could not afford the tuition. He had never given to the Seminary before but he announced a gift of fifty thousand dollars so that American Jewry should have spiritual leaders.

But the most important gift we can give our children is not money. We can give of ourselves while we are still alive. We can give our love, concern, and presence when we are needed most. We can exemplify those values that are precious to us, like honesty, sensitivity, and compassion. We can give our children our encouragement. We can let them know that we believe in them and, thereby, help them to make productive lives for themselves. We can give them of our faith in the face of despair and tragedy and let them know that there is a God in the world and that He will help us face whatever we have to face in life.

When we think of a will, we usually think of a complicated legal document, concerned with property and possessions. Such a will is important and each of us should write one. But a beautiful custom developed among Jews of writing a different kind of will: an Ethical Will, in which a parent expressed to the children his or her most precious values, by which he hoped the children would always be guided.

One of our congregants shared with me such an Ethical Will in poetic form written by her mother, which I would like to share with you.

*To My Children:*

When this letter you will see,
I no longer here will be.
I, at last, will be at rest,
With Him who truly loved me best.

My eyes are closed in my last sleep.
Please, for me, do not weep.
Remember me as I lived among you.
And as I lived my life, you will too.

My will by now shall have been read.
I cannot change it, for now I am dead.

But, if a mistake has been made.
Correct it among you, so all can be paid.

You all were faithful to us in Life.
If what is left helps to ease the strife
Of the daily living which will be yours,
Rest in Peace, will then be ours.

Live at Peace with one another.
Help when in need, a sister or brother.
Envy not others their material gain.
But see to it that your good name
Is that of which you are most proud.
And all can proclaim it always, out loud.

Train your children in the way they should go.
Of their heritage and Judaism too, they should know.
The love of Torah and the Ten Commandments their guide.
And their Jewishness never should they hide.

Divide among you my trinkets and such.
Each had its memory though it may not be much.
My clothes can be given to those whom they'll fit.
My afghans you'll use and you'll perhaps see me knit,

When you close your eyes and dream of the past,
As I did so often here towards the last.
I leave you all that I had left.
I go to those of whom I was bereft.
The world will treat you well, my dears.
Have Faith in God and have no fears.

As we watched over you in Life, each sister and brother.
In Heaven again, we'll be Father and Mother
And watch you all from our Home above
Blessing you daily with our Love.
All my love,<br>MOTHER

At *Yizkor*, we recall those whom we loved, not for how much they left us in their wills but for the precious memories, the treasured moments, and the eternal values by which they lived. May we provide the same kind of memories for those who love us most, who look to us as exemplars for their own lives.

# 25.
# Taking an Incomplete

The writer and college professor Mary Kay Blakely wrote an essay recently in which she discussed the college phenomenon of students asking teachers for permission to postpone the taking of their final exams and, instead of receiving a grade for the class, taking an *incomplete*. She envies the fact that students can do this and imagines how delightful it would be if all of us could do the same thing.

For example, if you are late in arriving at the office because you have been bucking traffic, you simply say to your employer, "Please don't consider me late today. I'll take an *incomplete*."

Or, if you interview for a job and you are very nervous and you can't seem to get the words out and you know you have made a poor impression, you simply say to the personnel manager, "I'd like to take an *incomplete*."

Or, if you happen to be at a dinner party where the subjects range from foreign affairs to raising children, and people share countless half-baked opinions, instead of joining the discussion, you say, "I don't have an opinion yet. I'll take an *incomplete*."

Or, if you have been a candidate in an election and you have worked hard for many months and you lose, you simply say to the electorate, "I'll take an *incomplete*."

Or, if you happen to be a rabbi, the Jewish calendar tests you regularly. First comes *Rosh Hashanah*, then *Yom Kippur*, and then *Sukkot*, and a few Sabbaths in between for good measure. Along comes *Shemini Atzeret* and on *Shemini Atzeret* you rise before the congregation and say, "Dear friends, today I'd like to take an *incomplete*."

Wouldn't it be great if we could be like those college students, and whenever the going gets really rough we simply take an *incomplete*!

The possibilities are mind-boggling. Imagine what this strategy could do for our relationships. As husbands and wives, we sometimes think back and remember the crises between us. We fought over children, money, and vacations. We recall the anger and tension between us. Ah, if only we could take an *incomplete* and do it over again. We could focus more on each other's needs and remember that we often inflict hurt upon the person we love most.

As parents, we remember the fights between us and our children. We were just learning how to deal with them when they were in elementary school and suddenly they became teenagers. We were just beginning to cope with their adolescent *meshugaasen* and suddenly they were getting married. We were never really ready for each new stage in their development. If only we could go back and ask them for an *incomplete.*

Why do college students ask professors for an *incomplete?* They probably could get a *B* in the course, but they want an *A.* They want perfection! How different the real world is from college. In the real world none of us achieves perfection. At work, we make mistakes all the time. In our relationships, we often alienate the people we love most. In our morality, we make compromises that fall short of our ideals. In our Jewishness, we leave so many *mitzvot* undone. In our giving, we could give so much more *tzedakah* and help so many more people and so many great causes. After college, none of us achieves perfection.

But even at college, even those students who have taken an *incomplete,* must inevitably take a final examination in order to graduate. And *Yizkor* is a reminder that each of us must also one day take a final examination. When our life draws to a close, we will be judged by others, by our peers, by our loved ones, by God Himself. And, on that day, there will be no postponements and we won't be able to ask for an *incomplete.* Most of us will not get *A*'s because none of us is perfect. As *Kohelet,* Ecclesiastes, the book our Tradition prescribes for our reading this day, puts it: *"Ki adam eyn tzadik baaretz asher yaaseh tov v'lo yechta"*—For there is no man on earth so righteous who does only good and never sins. Many of us are too critical of our loved ones instead of appreciating them as precious gifts that have been loaned to us. Some of us impose our needs upon our children, instead of encouraging them to fulfill their own potential. Some of us are insensitive to the feelings of others because we are too preoccupied with our own feelings to be able to consider theirs. Some of us are not always honest in our dealings with others, with our employers, with our employees, with merchants. Though we ourselves are imperfect, we usually demand that others be perfect. All of these imperfections will be judged on our Final Examination.

But our Final Examination will be different. What will count most will not be like college where we have to demonstrate how much we have learned and how much we can recall and repeat. With our Final, what will count most is the effort we have expended. Our marriage may not be perfect, but most of the time we tried to be a good spouse, to encourage each other, to protect each other from the cold and callous world outside our home. Our children may not have turned out exactly as we had hoped, but God knows, we tried our best to give them an education and decent values in order to help them make worthwhile lives for themselves. We were not as honest and ethical as we should have been, but most of us tried to do what was right. We were sometimes weak and we sinned, but even when we sinned, we felt guilty and we determined to do better.

At college, the teachers vary. Some are understanding, others unfeeling. But the Teacher of Teachers is *eyl rachum v'chanun*—He is a compassionate and merciful God. He will understand us and He will empathize with our frailties.

On that day of our Final Exam, He will say to us, "You were imperfect, my child, you know it as well as I. I can't give you an *incomplete*; it's too late for that. But I know that you worked hard at life. You struggled to be a good spouse, a caring parent, an honest worker. You really tried to be a *Mentch*. Be assured that your effort was not wasted. I have watched you carefully because you are my precious child. Each day of your life I loved you, protected you, and worried about you. And now that your life on earth is coming to a close, do not be afraid of death. For as you return your soul to Me, I will continue to cherish you and care for you and be with you to all eternity."

# 26.
# The Secret of a Long Life

People are always seeking the secret of a long life. Often, in the newspaper, we read interviews of very old people whom the reporter inevitably asks, "To what do you attribute your longevity?"

In the Talmud, the same question is asked of Rabbi Nehunya ben Hakanah, who lived to a ripe old age. His disciples asked him:

*Bahmeh heerachta yamim?*
"To what do you ascribe your long life?"

I would like to share Rabbi Nehunya's answer with you to see if it might be of help to us in our own lives.

First, he said:

*Miyamay lo nitkabadti biklon chaveri:*
"I never sought respect through the derogation of another person."

In other words, he was always very careful not to embarrass another person. Rabbi Nehunya knew very well the many teachings of our Tradition, warning us against embarrassing another human being.

In the Talmud, it is written:

*Im hayah baal teshuvah al yomar lo zechor maasecha harishonim:*
"If a man is a penitent, you must not say to him: 'Ah, I remember you when . . .'"

When a person is trying to change his life, it is forbidden to use his past in order to embarrass him.

At the end of *Birkat Hamazon*, Grace after the Meal, we sing the words of the Psalmist:

*Naar hayiti gam zakanti v'lo rahiti tzadik neezav u'zaro mevakesh lachem:*
"I was young; I became old; but I never saw a righteous person who was forsaken, whose children had to beg for bread."

Our Tradition suggests that we sing those words very softly lest we embarrass a poor person who is sharing our meal with us and who will be embarrassed by those words.

The Rabbis of the Talmud express their abhorrence of embarrassing another in the strongest possible terms when they say:

*Kol hamalbin p'nei chavero barabim k'ilu shofech damim:*
"He who embarrasses another person publicly is as though he has shed his blood!"

And yet, are we not often guilty of this sin? In school we call a classmate by a nickname which may call attention to a defect that is painfully embarrassing. There are teachers who use sarcasm as a weapon to intimidate and humiliate students. At social gatherings husbands and wives will use each other as a butt for their humor, which can be very embarrassing to the victim as well as to the guests who are present.

What happens to a person when I embarrass him? It diminishes him as a person; it decreases his own worth in his own eyes; it makes him less capable of fulfilling his real potential.

A boy at college told me about his roommate during his freshman year. He criticized everything he did, laughed at him, ridiculed him. By the end of the year, this young man told me he could hardly tie his shoelaces without feeling that he was inept, bumbling, incapable of doing anything.

By constantly embarrassing another person, we can destroy him.

Why do I need to embarrass another? Perhaps because of my own inadequacy, my need to raise my own self-respect at somebody else's expense. Perhaps it indicates how little confidence I possess, how little I respect myself, how small and petty I can be.

Rabbi Nehunya lived long because he knew his own worth. He did not have to enhance his own stature by trampling upon the dignity of other people.

Then Rabbi Nehunyah went on to give a second reason why he had enjoyed longevity. He said:

*Vatran b'mamoni hayiti:*
"I was generous with my money."

How well Rabbi Nehunyah understood what money can do to shorten a person's life. In the drive for money some people forget they have families. In that same quest some are willing to break any law or statute. For some, it means neglecting their health and in the process developing ulcers, heart disease, or high blood pressure. For some people, the desperate desire for money can be destructive of their own lives.

And the kind of battles that can develop over money. Sometimes, if children are not happy with the terms of a parent's will, they can become lifelong enemies, and a family can be destroyed.

Even in marriage, where two people love each other very much, they may have serious disagreements over money. There are some people who use money as a weapon with which to control their partner. There are some couples where one partner has great difficulty in spending money and the other finds it impossible to save money.

I saw a couple like that recently. The husband had lived through the Depression as a child but now makes a good living. Yet he continues to live with the same penuriousness as if he were still living in the Depression. The wife, on the other hand, had a very stingy mother and as a young girl growing up was always embarrassed because she had only one dress and was compelled to wear it every day. Now she has a closetful of dresses, more than she can use. She is a compulsive spender, married to a husband who lives in a perpetual Depression, a combination that bodes poorly for the future of their marriage.

Perhaps the starkest example of the strange attitudes people exhibit toward money was that of a man who died a few years ago, known as the richest miser in the world. He was the Nizam of Hyderabad, India, and his annual income was fifty million dollars. He had three wives and forty-two concubines and so many children that he once said he had never bothered to count them. He spent his leisure hours dipping his arms up to the elbows in chests full of diamonds, emeralds, rubies, and pearls. He possessed a fleet of Cadillacs and Rolls-Royces. But he himself always rode around in an old battered Ford. He planned the palace menus very carefully each day in order to guard against any frivolous spending. He always dressed in old, crumpled clothes and scuffed shoes, and he slept in a small room. He passed the time writing poetry and fending off his numerous kinsmen who constantly begged him for money, requests to which he never responded.

He even refused to pay any bills incurred by his wives when they went shopping. Whatever they brought into the palace, he would order returned to the stores immediately.

How very different was Rabbi Nehunyah and his approach to money. He understood that the person who is able to give of his money to a good cause, to a Synagogue, a Seminary, a Day School, to Israel, has the pleasure of seeing his money achieve great things, which adds interest and meaning to his life.

Erich Fromm once put it this way: "In the sphere of material things, giving means being rich. Not he who has much is rich, but he who gives much. The hoarder who is anxiously worried about losing something is, psychologically speaking, the poor impoverished man, regardless of how much he has. Whoever is capable of giving of himself is rich."

Finally, Rabbi Nehunyah added a third reason for his longevity:

*V'lo alta al mitati killat chaveri:*
"I never went to sleep thinking of a curse against another person."

In other words, Rabbi Nehunyah was the kind of person who simply could not bear a grudge against another.

There are some people who specialize in grudges. There are the people with memories like elephants—they never forget anything, particularly a slight, an insult, a fight. Long after you have forgotten the incident, they remember it vividly and in detail. They carry the grudge with them forever; they nurse it; they cultivate it; they help it to grow until it becomes like a cancer, eating away at their souls. It embitters their lives; it fills them with anger and resentment; it stays with them always; they find that at times it will not let them sleep, eat, or enjoy life. They will often stay away from a Bar Mitzvah, a wedding, a *simcha*, to show their anger, not realizing that in the process they are depriving themselves of life's most treasured moments!

Do you want to live long? says Rabbi Nehunyah. Then do not permit yourself to harbor grudges. You will be much happier and so will everybody else who has dealings with you.

# Growing Jewishly

# 1.
# A Strategy for Jewish Renewal

On these great days of *Rosh Hashanah* and *Yom Kippur*, we will be praying and hearing about vital themes in human life, about sin, repentance, God, the possibility of making a new beginning in our lives. How do we give these themes lasting import so that they will have a genuine impact on our lives; so that they will make a difference in the way we live?

Let me tell you what a group of Hasidim used to do, to see if we can adopt their strategy for ourselves. These were Hasidim of the Bratzlaver Rebbe, a rabbi who flourished at the end of the eighteenth century in the Ukraine. A group of his Hasidim who lived in Lodz, Poland, created a group, a *chevra*, among themselves which they called *"Chevra Shomrey Mishpat"*—Guardians of Justice.

The *Chevra* had a special journal, a kind of calendar-diary for the entire year. At the end of each day, each member of the group would make an entry—a check mark next to each of several questions—writing Yes or No to indicate whether he had fulfilled a particular obligation.

What were the questions? The first question was: Did you say the *Shema* today? Why did they choose the Shema? Because it is the single most important prayer of the entire Jewish liturgy. Why is it so important? Because it reminds a Jew each day of his life as he says its words: *"Shema Yisrael Adonay Eloheynoo Adonay Echad"*—I believe that there is a God in the world.

That belief has many implications. It means that God insists that we live by His teachings and that there is a difference between right and wrong, moral and immoral, regardless of how many would like to ignore those differences.

It means that there is a God in the world and that He endows us with countless blessings for which we should give Him thanks.

It affirms that there is a God in the world and He gives us strength when we need it most, in times of trouble and despair. There is a special Psalm we read each day during the month preceding *Rosh Hashanah*, in which the Psalmist affirms his faith in God by saying: *"Kee avi v'imi azavoonee vadonai yaasfeynee"*—Even if my father and mother were to abandon me, my God would take me in. Our God will never abandon any of His children.

The first question they had to answer was: Did you recite the *Shema* and did you remember that there is a God in the world.

They had to answer a second question, which was: Did you study Torah today? Did you study the *Shulchan Aruch*? The Mishnah? The Talmud? They knew that in Judaism there is no way to faith other than through study. Because if you don't study Torah, how will you know what God requires of you? They knew that in our religion there are simply no shortcuts to faith; there is no instant Judaism. To be a Jew requires a lifetime of study.

In our High School of Jewish Studies, I read a story to my students entitled *"Titchadesh"* by David Frishman. *Titchadesh* is a word we use in congratulating a person who is wearing a new garment. This story is about an impoverished boy who dreams of the day when he would acquire a new garment so that people would say to him, like they did to everybody else, *"Titchadesh."* He becomes ill and nobody ever says the word to him until the moment he lies dying. Then he sees angels hovering above him and saying to him, *"Titchadesh."*

The students were deeply moved by this story and one of the girls said to me, "How come we never heard of this writer in Hebrew School?" I replied, "You can't cover everything in Hebrew School. That's why we have a high school and that's why a Jew never stops studying if she is to discover for herself the treasures of Jewish literature and tradition."

Each person had to answer a third question: Did you give *tzedaka* today? Under the category of *tzedaka* they asked if the Hasid had made a contribution to help publish the Rabbi's writings. If you believe in somebody and his teachings, you want to help spread the word so others might benefit as well.

But you were supposed to give *tzedaka* for other good causes as well. For *tzedaka* is the Jewish method to right some of the wrongs that the world inflicts upon human beings. Danny Siegel is an idealistic young man, a poet, and activist, who has made *tzedaka* his special *mitzvah*. In order to personalize the giving of *tzedaka*, he asks for contributions and then he seeks out people in Israel who are doing good work by helping others. If you send Danny a contribution, at the end of the year he sends you a *tzedaka* report, detailing the *tzedaka* he has distributed.

One example of his giving is to a woman whose name is Esther Segal (not related to him) who lives in Jerusalem. Seventeen years ago her doctors said her physical condition was hopeless. At that time she promised herself that if she recovered, she would devote her life to *tzedaka* and *gmilut hasadim*. She recovered and she works in three major areas: she provides free loans to people with no interest; she gives *tzedaka*, money which she does not expect to have returned; and she helps young couples and poor brides who need help. Esther Segal is a one-woman social service agency. A Jew not only gives *tzedaka*. He should always be searching for new ways to make his giving more effective and more life-enhancing.

Those Bratzlaver Hasidim had to answer another question: Did you dance today? They did not mean social dancing or folk dancing. They were referring to the special dance of Hasidic Jews during the Service or at the very end of the Service. The founder of Hasidism, Israel Baal Shem Tov, taught: "The dances of the Jew before his Creator are prayers, for it is written in the Book of Psalms: '*Kol atzmotay tomarnah Adonai mi chamocha*'—All my limbs proclaim: Who is like unto You, O Lord?" It is an attempt by Hasidim to achieve the qualities of *hitlahavut*, religious ecstasy, and *deveykut*, communion with God.

In Israel, when we pray at the *Kotel* on Friday evening, the students of Yeshivat Hakotel dance in a large circle before the *Kotel*. Our people are usually hesitant to enter the dancing circle because they are unfamiliar with this phenomenon. I urge them to join the circle, and when they do they love the experience. They begin to understand how dance can also be an expression of love for God.

The next question they had to answer was: Did you have *sichat haverim* today; did you have a discussion with a friend? They wanted to know if you had discussed the Rabbi's teachings together with another person. They understood the need people have for strengthening each other in their convictions.

That is why people become part of different groups to rid

themselves of undesirable habits, like Weight Watchers, or Smoke Enders, or Alcoholics Anonymous. It is why people join groups to help them in their resolve to improve themselves, like *Havurot*, like friends celebrating *Shabbat* or *Yom Tov* together. It is the reason these Hasidim created this *Chevra Shomrey Mishpat*.

*Sichat chaverim* was intended for another purpose as well. It meant: did you encourage another person when he needed your help? For after all, what good is all your learning and observance unless you are willing to help another person in trouble, such as visiting a person who is ill, or comforting a person who is bereaved, or encouraging a person who is depressed.

The final question they asked was: Did you practice *hitbodedut*, solitude, today? How were you supposed to use this solitude? It was intended to give a person time to express his innermost feelings.

Each one of us needs to spend some time by ourselves each day. A mother needs a little time for herself, away from screaming children. At work, we often feel hemmed in by unceasing tension and we need some moments of surcease. A teenager who is always aware of peer pressure about him needs some time to ask himself: What do I really feel and want as an individual? Each of us needs *hitbodedut*, a little space for ourselves each day.

They saw another reason for *hitbodedut*. It was an opportunity to converse with God about one's innermost longings and hopes. We need some time each day away from everybody, to think about what is happening to us and what we really want to accomplish with our lives.

In addition, *hitbodedut* gave a person time to confess his sins before God and to determine to improve his conduct. Each of us sins. We wrong others so often with our words and our actions. Each day we should make a *cheshbon hanefesh*—an accounting of the soul—and try to see how we can make amends and do better the next day. And when should this *hitbodedut* take place? The Bratslaver Rabbi suggested that it should be done at night, when the house is quiet, when everybody has gone to sleep. Those are the quiet moments you need to learn more about yourself and the meaning and purpose of your life.

Well, what do you think? Would you consider using the Bratslaver Hasidim's strategy for yourself? If you form a *chevra* or *chavurah* with whom to do it, it will be easier because you will be able to encourage one another. Or perhaps you would like to make your family into a *chevrah* for using this strategy. Or perhaps you want to do it by yourself. In any case, get yourself a calendar-diary and next to each day, write these six questions:

1. Did you recite the *Shema* today?
2. Did you study Torah today?
3. Did you give *tzedaka*?
4. Did you dance and try to achieve religious ecstasy?
5. Did you spend some time helping another person?
6. Did you practice *hitbodedut*, a few moments of solitude, communing with God about the meaning of your life?

Such a strategy can make *Rosh Hashanah* and *Yom Kippur* have a lasting impact upon our lives. Such a strategy can transform us into fully committed and observant Jews.

# 2.
# What *Yom Kippur* Can Do for You

Rabbi Israel Salanter, the founder of the Musar Movement in the nineteenth century, taught some special teachings about the High Holy Days which can have a profound meaning for each of us on these great days.

First, he said:

> *Af b'shaah she'atah yarey v'nifchad me'eymat hadin, eyn atta patur meylhizaheyr l'val tidroch al regel chavercha.*
> "Even while you are absorbed in concern and trepidation about the Day of Judgment, you are not free to violate the prohibition against stepping on another person's toes."

Imagine for yourself a small synagogue in Europe with very limited space for each person. As a person became very involved in prayer, moving his body back and forth, there was always the possibility of stepping on another's feet. Therefore, Rabbi Israel said: "Your absorption in your prayers is no excuse for forgetting another person's needs."

One of the critical moments in Martin Buber's life happened as he was absorbed in mystical contemplation of God. He was visited by a young boy who was about to enter the army. Buber heard what he had to say but he really didn't "listen" to what he was saying. Subsequently, the young man committed suicide. When Buber heard about his death, he was shattered. He felt that if he had truly listened to him, he might have saved his life. From that emotional trauma came a rethinking by Buber of his whole philosophy of life and a new understanding of the I-Thou relationship—the need for a genuine concern for each person.

One year, Rabbi Salanter became ill before Passover. He was, therefore, unable to supervise the women who were baking the *matzot*. His students who offered to take his place asked him what they should watch for. They thought he would emphasize many of the stringent Passover laws. Instead, he replied: "See to it that the women are paid adequately."

There is a danger which is ever present in religion. People who are observant can begin to feel superior to those who are less observant. They may look down upon them, make derogatory comments about them, assuming that they are much closer to God. Rabbi Israel would say to them: "Don't let your interest in Judaism blind you to the needs or feelings of another." Through love and acceptance we may bring a person closer to Judaism. Through denigration we will drive him away.

Rabbi Israel Salanter offered a second teaching:

> *Kesheomedet lefanecha sheylah l'veyrur, dan otah lefi hacheshbon: eych hayita noheyg b'shaat Neilah b'Yom haKipurim.*
> "When you have to make a decision, ask yourself: 'How would I decide if it were *Neilah* on *Yom Kippur*?' "

The *Neilah* Service on *Yom Kippur* is a time of great solemnity which is felt by each Jew. It is, after all, the last opportunity for penitence before the Gates of Heaven are closed, before the Book of Judgment is sealed. If we had to make an ethical decision at that moment, each of us would do better than during the rest of the year. Rabbi Israel says: We need to try to re-create this moment whenever we make decisions.

Each time a physician makes a decision, it can lead to health or illness, life or death for the patient. A journalist may reveal a story that can destroy a person's reputation and his life. An editor who decides whether or not to publish a person's poem, essay, or story is making a critical decision for the writer. Even if he decides to reject the offering, the response can be written with cruelty or compassion. A businessman making a deal faces many complicated ethical dilemmas. A personnel manager who decides to hire a person may be giving him a chance at life. When he has to fire a worker, he may be destroying his career. A teacher deciding to pass or fail a student is making an important decision.

In our own families, as spouses, we sometimes make decisions about each other which are critical, such as should we keep our marriage going or should we break up.

Parents and children make momentous decisions about each other. We sometimes have to decide whether we should encourage our child in a career which we have not chosen for him. When our parents become older, we have to determine whether we shall encourage their autonomy or make them more dependent upon us. Whenever you make a decision, teaches Rabbi Israel, ask yourself the question: "How would I decide if it were *Neilah* on *Yom Kippur*?"

Finally, Rabbi Salanter taught a third teaching to all of us:

*Haolam noheyg lashuv bitshuvah bimey haslichot. anshey maaseh makdimim lashuv b'chodesh Elul. vaani omeyr: sheyeysh l'hatchil bitshuvah techef acharey N'eelat Yom haKipurim.*
"People begin to do *teshuvah* during the days of *Slichot*. The more devout begin earlier, during the month of Elul. But my view is that *teshuvah* has to begin immediately after *Neilah* on *Yom Kippur*."

What usually destroys the effect of *Yom Kippur* on our lives? We listen to the words of the liturgy and the sermons and we say: "It makes sense. It's a good idea, but not now. I'm too busy. When the *Slichot* days come, then I'll start thinking seriously about the meaning of my life." Others, who are more devout, don't wait for *Slichot* but begin with *Rosh Hodesh Elul*, a whole month before the High Holy Days. But Rabbi Israel insists: Both efforts are not good enough. Procrastination will destroy the best of intentions. You must begin *teshuvah* right after *Neilah*—now! Do you want to observe more *mitzvot*? You have to begin now! Do you want to become more sensitive to others? You have to start now! Do you want to make your decisions more ethical, more honest, more holy? You must begin— now! If you begin now, this *Yom Kippur* can become the most important day of your life.

# 3.
# Why We Survived

The *sukkah* is rich in symbolic meanings and they serve as a kind of paradigm of Jewish history. Our history has been very much like a *sukkah*. We had a frail, uncertain existence and our fate was blasted by every wind of man's hatred. Yet, somehow, we are here, and our little *sukkah* is still here.

In the Louvre Museum in Paris there is a great archeological treasure which is approximately three thousand years old. It is called the Moabite Stone and was erected by Mesha, King of Moab. On it are inscribed these boastful words:

> As for Omri, king of Israel, he humbled Moab many years, for Chemosh [the god of Moab] was angry at his land. And his son followed him and he also said: 'I will humble Moab.' In my time he spoke thus, but I have triumphed over Omri, king of Israel, and over his house, while Israel hath perished for ever.

His boast was somewhat premature. As it happens, not only has Moab disappeared, but some of the greatest empires, Assyria, Babylonia, Rome, who at one time or another dominated our people, have also disappeared. Their monuments have disintegrated and their power has dissipated. Yet we are here and our frail *sukkah* is still here.

Why? Why, indeed, are we still here? First, because of our unfaltering belief in God and our belief that He was not defeated. We were defeated because we deserved to be defeated but not God. Generally, ancient peoples, when they suffered defeat, believed that their god had been conquered. But not our people. Our prophets interpreted our defeat as being the result of our own immoral and unethical behavior. They taught our ancestors that we sinned against God and against men and, therefore, He punished us by exiling us from our land.

The *musaf* prayer we recite today says:

*Umipney chataeynu galinu me'artzeynu:*
"Because of our sins we were exiled from our land."

There is another reason why we are still here. We are here because of the Torah. We always believed that the Torah contains God's teachings, and those teachings guided us, nourished our spirits, and sustained our souls. Regardless of our difficult physical existence, regardless of the libels of our enemies, we were secure in the knowledge that we were trying with all our hearts to live by God's word. Through Torah we learned the meaning of a beautiful round of ritual, a great faith, a demanding and exalting system of ethics that gave meaning and purpose to our lives.

We are here, too, because we always kept alive our historic consciousness as a people. We never really felt totally isolated. We read the stories of our people and lived with our great forefathers, David, Judah Maccabee, and Bar Kochba. We celebrated our Holy Days and felt ourselves to be an integral part of Israel of the past and of the Jewish people of the present.

On Passover, at the Seder, we relived our bondage and our Exodus from Egypt together with all Jews. On *Sukkot* we relived the wandering of our people in the wilderness, sharing their dream of the Promised Land, and we dwelt in frail tabernacles with them along the way.

Physically, we were as frail as a *sukkah*, but spiritually, if a cold blast of hatred destroyed our temporary dwelling, we could always pick ourselves up from the ruins and move on to create a new home, with the hope that it would have more permanence the next time. The history of the Jewish people is symbolized by the *sukkah*.

In truth, not only the history of our people but, in a certain sense, the life of each person can be compared to the *sukkah* because our sojourn on earth is so temporary and so transitory. Each of us is here for such a brief time. In the words of the Psalmist: "The days of our years are three score years and ten; or even by reason of strength, four score years."

If this is so, the question arises: Why do we engage in spending our days as if we were going to live forever, amassing, striving, and struggling for more means, more possessions, more security? Why are we so reluctant to do *mitzvot* while we are here? We cannot postpone doing the right things forever. We are, after all, on this earth only for a very short time.

The *sukkah* says to each person: Don't put off all the good resolves you were planning. If you were going to say something decent to an employee, don't put it off. If you were planning to participate more actively with your faith and your people, don't put it off. Each of us lives in a bodily *sukkah*, a temporary abode, for a very short time. Whatever good we hope to accomplish we had better begin today.

Remember how the poet put it:

> I shall pass through this world but once.
> Any good therefore that I can do
> Or any kindness that I can show
> To any human being
> Let me do it now. Let me
> Not defer or neglect it for
> I shall not pass this way again.

In truth, an even greater miracle occurred in the course of Jewish history. Our people not only survived, but even more miraculously we never turned into a wandering band of gypsies and vagabonds. Instead, we gave birth to prophets, saints, sages, and scholars. We created a vast literature, of philosophy, poetry, law, and ethics. We produced great physicians, scientists, and artists. We have enriched, far beyond our numbers, the spiritual heritage of mankind.

How did we accomplish all this? Jewish law says that the *sukkah* must have a thatched roof that is not too thick, to enable a person to look up at the heavens and see the stars. Despite man's inhumanity, despite his propensity to wreak havoc and fight senseless wars, the Jewish people proclaimed to mankind a vision of man's ultimately achieving peace:

> They shall not hurt nor destroy
> In all My holy mountain;
> For the earth shall be full of the
> knowledge of the Lord,
> As the waters cover the sea.

Despite men's hatred of each other, despite their denial of the unity of mankind, the Jewish people proclaimed a vision of men one day recognizing that God is One and that all men are one:

And the Lord shall be King over all the earth;
In that day shall the Lord be One and His name One.

Despite men's fears and terrors, the Jewish people proclaimed a vision of men one day living free, secure, and unafraid:

"They shall sit, every man under his vine and under his fig-tree; And none shall make them afraid . . ."

Our people had a vision of a better world, and therefore we continued to exist and to enhance the life of mankind.

As we enter the *sukkah* today, may we be inspired to renew our own faith in God, our own love for His Torah, our own identification with our people, our own dream and vision of a world of which even its Creator may yet one day find great reason to be proud.

# 4.
# The Art of Forgiveness

*Yom Kippur* offers each of us a very special gift. It is a unique day which tries to teach us a very difficult but precious quality, the art of forgiveness. I would like to talk with you today about that rare but essential attitude in human life.

Usually, when we think of *Yom Kippur*, we think of a day when we ask God for forgiveness. But today I would like to suggest that instead we use this *Yom Kippur* to try to forgive God.

It sounds strange, doesn't it? It sounds like real *chutzpah* that we should forgive God! Yet I would submit that this is a vital necessity for many of us. We need to forgive God because many of us are alienated from Him. Sometimes we are estranged from Him because of our parents' authoritarianism, their rigidity in communicating Judaism to us. We resent what they imposed upon us and we continue to fight them and "their" God. Some of us have had bad experiences with a Hebrew school or with a teacher, and they turned us away from God. Some of us had a professor in college who delighted in destroying our faith and who gave us nothing to fill the vacuum.

In addition, we need to forgive God because many of us are angry with Him. We are angry because of the suffering of good friends, or the death of someone we loved.

A man once told me that he was thirteen years old when his father died. After that tragic loss, he would never enter a synagogue again.

We need to forgive God because many of us are disillusioned with Him. We are disillusioned because of the death of six million of our brothers and sisters in the Holocaust. We want to know where He was when a million innocent Jewish children died in that inferno.

What will enable us to forgive God? We have to rid ourselves of our misrepresentations of Him and instead struggle to achieve a more mature understanding of Him. Despite the misrepresentations of Him by parents and teachers and philosophers, our Tradition teaches us that our God is not rigid, cruel, or indifferent. Despite our misconceptions of Him, He does not cause premature death, He does not cause auto or plane accidents, He does not pollute the environment. No, our God is *Eyl rachum v'chanun*. He is patient, compassionate, and loving, but His reputation is often most damaged by those who seek to represent Him. Our God gives us the gift of life and He wants us to live well and fully, but He offers us no guarantees. He grieves with us when we lose a loved one, and He suffers with us when we suffer. He regrets our polluting the environment and our destroying the beautiful world He gave us to inhabit and to enhance. He mourns with us the deaths of the six million, who were murdered because of demoniac people who led a willing nation and because of a world that remained indifferent to Jewish suffering. The better we understand God and His love for us, the more possible it will become for us to forgive Him.

On this day of *Yom Kippur* we are usually taught that we must ask others for forgiveness, and that is true and essential. But, today, I would like to emphasize instead the need for each of us to learn to forgive others.

We need to forgive those who have hurt us at work, our employer who has wounded us by a cutting remark and a fellow-worker who insulted us by a hostile glance. We need to forgive our friends, who failed us when we needed them. Husbands and wives need to forgive each other for the hurt they have inflicted by not paying enough attention to each other's feelings. We accumulate these hurts, we brood about them, and we see no hope for our relationships that have been broken.

How can we overcome our anger and resentment and learn to forgive others? We need to cultivate a greater understanding of other people's existential situation. The cutting remark may come from a person who is himself suffering. It's really no excuse but it may give us some insight into the situation. When a friend fails us, we have to ponder the agony with which he himself may be struggling. When our spouse fails to listen to us, perhaps it is because he or she is preoccupied with his or her own worries.

There is an old Welsh folksong that expresses the difficulty in understanding another's pain. It says: "My heart moves as heavy as the horse that climbs a hill, and I can't for my dear life pretend to be happy. You know nothing of the place where my shoe is pinching. And many, many troubled thoughts are quite breaking my heart."

The better we understand others and their own situations, the more likely it is that we will be able to forgive them.

So far we have spoken of forgiveness which is directed to others. On this day I want to also emphasize the importance of forgiving ourselves. Most of us torment ourselves with feelings of self-condemnation. The renowned psychologist Carl Rogers writes: "If I were to search for the central core of difficulty in people as I have come to know them, it is that in the great majority of cases they despise themselves, regarding themselves as worthless and unlovable."

We cannot forgive ourselves for the things that go wrong in life. If our marriage is broken, we berate ourselves and ask, "Why didn't I act differently?" If our children are in trouble or not doing well, we torment ourselves, asking, "What did I do wrong?" If we make a wrong decision, we punish ourselves and ask, "How could I have been so stupid?" If a loved one dies, we flagellate ourselves with the thought, "I should never have said the terrible things I said." We torture ourselves with feelings of self-recrimination and self-denigration.

On this *Yom Kippur*, how can we learn to forgive ourselves? We have to develop a greater understanding of ourselves and our own limitations. It is, of course, a basic teaching of *Yom Kippur* that where we have sinned against others, we must recompense them and attempt reconciliation with them. But we also need to recognize that we are frail and fallible human beings. Most of us usually do our best in life, but some things are beyond our control. Broken marriages may happen despite our best intentions. Children may develop problems even with the most caring parents. Even the wisest people make mistakes.

*Mazel* is also a very important factor in life and we don't all receive an equal share of *mazel*. We also need to remind ourselves that no human relationships are perfect. When a loved one dies, we regret the arguments we had and the harsh words we used. But we need to remind ourselves that all of these are part of the normal tensions of even the most loving relationships. We have a wonderful God and He reassures us on *Yom Kippur* and says that if only we will repent with sincerity, He will respond by saying to each one of us, "*Salachti*"—I forgive you, my child. And as He forgives us, so must we learn to forgive ourselves.

Do you want this day to have a lasting impact on your lives? Then cultivate the gift of forgiveness.

Forgive God and welcome Him back into your life and, thereby, find a new world of strength and comfort.

Forgive others and rid yourself of the anger and hurt that seethe within you and embitter your life.

Forgive yourself by turning away from the anguish of the past and turn instead to the work of fashioning a new and brighter future.

# 5.
# How to Celebrate a Jewish *Simcha*

How do you celebrate a Jewish *simcha*? It is possible to learn a great deal about the method of celebrating a *simcha* from this Festival of Sukkot.

In describing *Sukkot*, it is remarkable that the Torah uses the word *simcha* three times, more than for any other festival. Rejoicing is clearly of the essence in celebrating this *Yom Tov*. As a matter of fact, in our liturgy, we call *Sukkot* "Zman Simchateynoo"—the time of our rejoicing.

Moses Maimonides, in his *Mishneh Torah*, gives some very specific teachings about how to celebrate a *Yom Tov* as a *simcha*. The first requisite, he says, is to celebrate with the family. You have to pay special attention to the children by giving them snacks and gifts. You should provide your wife with new outfits and jewelry, according to what you can afford. Your meals should be especially festive. For a Jewish *simcha*, you must celebrate together as a family.

*Sukkot* gives us some wonderful opportunities to fulfill that precept. We can build a *sukkah* together. We can help other families build a *sukkah* for themselves. We can go "*sukkah*-hopping" during *Chol Hamoed*.

This is true not only of *Sukkot*; it is true for every Holy Day, whether it be Passover, *Rosh Hashanah*, or *Shabbat*. Celebrating with the family gives the day special meaning and special pleasure. The truth is that we need to set aside time for family not only on Holy Days and *Shabbat*. A family can only flourish and feel like a family if its members spend some time together each day.

I was saddened to read a story in the *Boston Globe* recently about how many families no longer eat dinner together. Mary Lyons, for example, works for the Cambridge School Department. She works all day and is exhausted when she comes home. She prepares dinner for her husband and their three sons, and her husband and sons eat their dinners on trays in the den, watching TV. She says she is happy to eat dinner by herself at the kitchen table while she reads the newspaper and relaxes.

Dr. John Szlyk, a psychiatrist at Tufts New England Medical Center, asks those families who do not have dinner together if they do anything together. Do they play together, go shopping together, do anything together that will give them an opportunity to communicate?

If they don't, he says, "I have . . . prescribed reinstituting the family dinner hour." Imagine, today you have to be given a prescription to have dinner together! Dr. Szlyk explains why dinner together is so important: "Food is symbolic of nurturance, and the first activity between the infant and the world is eating. Later, the experience can continue to be about giving. The ritual of passing food from person to person, of sharing food and its preparation, can be rich emotionally. People need some emotional feeding at the end of the day. Children, especially, need to feel taken care of. God knows, they have to take care of themselves later."

We need to be together as a family, not only for a *simcha* but every day, so that we should develop an appreciation for the gift of being part of a family, of people who really care for each other.

There is a second requisite, according to Maimonides, which is essential to a Jewish *simcha*. He writes: "*Ooche'shehoo ocheyl v'shoteh, chayav l'haachil lageyr layatom v'lalmanah im shaar ha'aniyim haoomlalim*"—When a Jew eats and drinks at his festive meals, he must also provide food for the stranger, the orphan, and the widow, as well as for other deprived people. Furthermore, he adds: "He who locks his doors and eats together with his family only—*eyn zo simchat mitzvah elah simchat kreyso*"—this is not the *simcha* of a *mitzvah*; it is a *simcha* for his own stomach.

How does a Jew celebrate a *simcha*? He shares his blessings with others who do not possess his means.

I read a story recently about a lady in St. Petersburg, Florida, whose name was Mrs. Elsie DeFratus. She was nearly eighty years old, and she had survived for a long time on her meager widow's pension. She scrimped and saved, often skipping meals, eating less each day because of the rising costs of food until one morning she was found dead in her tiny apartment. She weighed seventy-six pounds. The coroner concluded that the cause of death was "malnutrition." But an elderly friend had another explanation. She said it was "surrender. She just stopped believing tomorrow would be better."

Maimonides would say to us that as long as there are people who are hungry in your land or in other countries of the world—if you can't bring them to your house, then at least give to organizations like CARE and OXFAM and others like them, to prevent them from dying of hunger.

If you celebrate a Bar Mitzvah or a wedding, and you spend a great deal of money on the meal, the flowers, and the music, then make certain that you also do an act of *tzedakah* at the same time, that will make it a *simcha shel mitzvah*. How does a Jew celebrate a *simcha*? Not only with his own family and friends but in helping to provide for those who have no friends.

Lest you think that a Jewish *simcha* consists only of eating and drinking—and you begin to feel that to be truly *froom* what you should do on *Yom Tov* is eat and drink all day, Maimonides makes it clear that such a regimen is inappropriate. Instead, he prescribes, in the morning you should go to the Synagogue to pray and listen to the Torah reading. Then you come home and have lunch; then you should return to the Synagogue to study Torah and pray and then you return home to eat again. The Jewish pattern of holiness includes sustenance for the body and the soul. A Jewish *simcha* has to include worship of God and study of His Torah. Furthermore, in this same pattern of holiness which he describes, even the eating and drinking at the *simcha* must be done in moderation. "*Shehashikroot v'haschok harabah, eynah simcha elah holeyloot v'sichloot*"—Drunkenness, excessive levity, and irreverence are not a *simcha* but can turn the entire occasion into a sham and a farce.

The Talmud tells a story about the wedding of the son of Rabbi Mar, son of Ravina. The host saw that the Rabbis and the other wedding guests were reaching a point of reckless abandon in their celebration. The only way he could attract their attention was by taking a precious crystal cup worth four hundred zuz and smashing it, and suddenly they all became serious. Then he reminded them that even at a *simcha*, a Jew must never lose his *tzelem elohim*, the image of God that gives him dignity and holiness as a human being.

When you celebrate a *simcha* in the manner I have described, whether it's a Holy Day like *Sukkot* or one of the rites of passage, or whenever you do a *mitzvah*, then of such a *simcha*, says Maimonides: *"Hasimcha sheyismach adam baasiyat hamitzvah . . .avodah gedolah hee"*— When you truly rejoice in the doing of a *mitzvah*, it becomes an exalted form of worship. It is one of the greatest ways to worship God.

Why does this Festival of *Sukkot* emphasize the importance of *simcha* so much? As long as we fulfill the *mitzvah*, what difference does our mood make?

Our Tradition understood that when we are sad, we have no room for anything else in our hearts but ourselves. All we can think of is our own ailments, problems, and troubles. Our obsessive concern with ourselves crowds out the possibility of reaching out to God and to His children.

But when we learn to rejoice in doing a *mitzvah*, on our Holy Days, on *Shabbat*, in our daily lives, then we suddenly find that something miraculous occurs. Rabbi Nachman of Bratzlav described it this way: *"Ah simcha efent oif dos hartz"*—Rejoicing opens up the heart. A *simcha* opens our hearts to our own families. It inspires us to love them more and care for them more.

A *simcha* opens our hearts to those who are friendless and stimulates in us a greater concern for their needs.

A *simcha* opens our hearts to God Himself. Instead of complaining our way through life, it reminds us to be grateful to Him for His blessings and miracles which are with us each moment of our lives.

# 6.
# Creating Great Jews

What would you do if somebody offered you a formula for making your children outstanding—a formula for becoming a great musician, or a great scientist, or a great athlete? Most of us would jump at the opportunity and many of us would probably be prepared to pay large sums of money to obtain such a formula. There is such a formula and I would like to share it with you.

At the University of Chicago there is a research project which has been studying one hundred outstanding people. They are concert pianists, Olympic swimmers, tennis players, and research mathematicians who reached the top of their fields between the ages of seventeen and thirty-five. This research team, under the leadership of Professor Benjamin Bloom, one of the outstanding educational researchers in our country, has identified several prerequisites aside from native gifts that are crucial in producing this kind of excellence.

The first requisite is having parents who greatly value and enjoy these fields themselves, whether it be music, sports, art, or intellectual activity. These parents view such activities as a natural part of their own lives, so that the child learns their "language" as easily as he or she learns to speak.

For example, the parents of a successful pianist liked listening to music themselves and bought their children records and musical toys. They sang together; they showed their children how to play and read notes. One mother recalled that she had given her daughter a toy piano, which she kept close to where the child played. The mother commented, "It wasn't any time before she could pick out songs herself. She could play twenty-five songs by the time she was four years old. If you have an instrument where they can get at it, they'll learn it."

The swimmers' parents were not thinking about the Olympics when they took their three-year-olds to pools or sports clubs. None of the parents was a professional athlete, but sports and outdoor recreation were "a regular part of family life." In one family, the love of physical activity was so great that the child's seventy-year-old grandmother walked six miles a day to an exercise class. It was taken for granted that everyone in the family would participate in athletics and the children usually learned to swim by about age four. The first characteristic of these excelling people is having parents who greatly value and enjoy these fields.

These parents have a second characteristic: they believe in the work ethic. The parents constantly drilled into their children the notion that "you always have to do the very best you are capable of, that anything less is not enough." They learned to work hard, a quality their teachers would prize later on.

The third characteristic of these outstanding people was having a first teacher who was warm and loving, who made the lessons fun and who lavished rewards freely. These first teachers were not highly sophisticated; they were just very good with children. One pianist recalled her first teacher: "She carried a big bag of Hershey bars and gold stars for the music, and I was crazy about this lady. All I had to do was play the right notes in the right rhythm and I got a Hershey bar." The first teacher is critically important.

A fourth condition present in each of these families was the great encouragement and enthusiasm the parents gave in response to their child's progress. As soon as the child began to show some proficiency, the parents would make a great fuss about it. The children soon recognized that such accomplishments brought them attention and praise. The parents also involved themselves in the learning process. Some of the parents attended lessons with their children, and nearly all of them supervised daily practice. Some of the pianists' parents took music lessons themselves.

It's interesting that none of these outstanding people was a child prodigy. They obviously had great potential but it was realized only because of the profound impact of their parents and teachers.

I found this to be a very exciting piece of research because it raised the question in my mind: What if somebody could provide us with a formula for creating outstanding Jews? This research suggests that there really is such a formula for each of us.

It says that if you want to create great Jews, you have to have parents who value Judaism greatly and who view it as a natural part of their lives. You need the kind of parents who work to create a

Jewish ambiance in their home through introducing the beauty of Jewish rituals, books, music, and art. You require parents who observe *Shabbat* and who make this beautiful day the high point of the week, a day that the family looks forward to with joyous anticipation. You need parents who pray each day by saying a blessing at a meal, who utter a prayer of thanksgiving upon rising, who recite the *shema* before going to sleep. Their children then see that prayer is an important part of their parents' lives. You have to have parents who come to the Synagogue every *Shabbat* and who bring their children from an early age, making the Synagogue an integral part of their lives from their earliest years.

To create great Jews, parents have to cherish their own Jewishness and make it an essential part of their own lives.

If we want to create Jews who excel in their Jewishness, there is a second prerequisite. We need parents who believe in the work ethic. We need parents who make certain that their children study Torah at a good Hebrew school or day school. We must have parents who treat their children's Jewish studies with the same seriousness as they do their secular studies. We require parents who encourage their children to learn more Jewish skills, such as Torah reading, how to lead a Service, how to conduct a Seder.

A mother in our congregation said to me recently, "In our family the kids can complain as much as they like but they know that most things are optional like music lessons or ballet, but Jewish education is never optional." We need parents who believe that you have to work at becoming a Jew.

To create a great Jew, you need a third requisite: the first teacher must be warm and loving, a teacher who makes Jewish study a positive and enjoyable experience. One week there was a beautiful array of posters in our Community Hall created by the youngsters of our Hebrew school. They were asked to depict their perception of Jerusalem. I was one of the judges and found it difficult to make a decision because of the beauty and creativity of the entries. There were First, Second, and Third Prizes in many categories, but everyone who entered the contest received a prize. Can you guess what it was? It was a Hershey bar!

There is one more ingredient necessary in the process of creating great Jews. We need the encouragement, enthusiasm, and involvement of the parents in response to their children's progress. We need parents who ask their children questions about their Jewish studies, who help them with their homework, who meet with their teachers to check on their progress. We require parents who make a fuss when their child learns something new and who are proud of a newly learned song or prayer or skill and who tell other members of the family about it. We must have parents who study Torah themselves, in a Hebrew Literacy Program, in an Adult Bar/Bat Mitzvah course, in an *ulpan* at the Hebrew College, in adult education courses.

In my former congregation I remember receiving an irate phone call from a mother who complained that we had taught her daughter to light candles for *Shabbat*. She told me she didn't want her daughter bringing home rituals from which she herself had escaped. Now that's what you call real enthusiasm on the part of a parent!

I began with the question: "What would you do if somebody were to offer you a formula for making your children outstanding—a great musician, or scientist, or athlete?" I suggested that most of us would respond with great enthusiasm even if it might be very costly.

Now, what about the second question I raised: "What if somebody could provide you with a formula for creating outstanding Jews?" What is your response? Are you saying to yourself, "That's too much effort," or That's unimportant," or "I've got other priorities that are more important." If that is your response, then don't be disappointed if you find that your children and grandchildren will have far less interest in being Jewish than you do and even if some of them decide to look elsewhere for spiritual nourishment—to other religions or cults or gurus as far as possible from their Jewish roots and their Jewish heritage.

I hope that each of us will have a different response. I hope we will say: more than anything else, we want our children and grandchildren to be Jews, to know the beauty, inspiration, and courage that comes from being a Jew. And, yes, we are willing to involve ourselves wholeheartedly in the process of creating great Jews, with study, work, and enthusiasm.

Our response can determine the future of our families and the destiny of our people.

# 7.
# Three Unusual Bar Mitzvahs

A Bar Mitzvah means very different things to different people. Each Bar Mitzvah has its own unique significance to the Bar Mitzvah boy, his family, and his friends. Today I would like to tell you about three very different kinds of Bar Mitzvahs and the special meanings they hold for their celebrants.

How do Israeli boys, living on a *kibbutz*, celebrate their Bar Mitzvah? If they live on a religious *kibbutz*, they celebrate it very much the way we do. They come to the Synagogue and are called to the Torah and Haftorah on *Shabbat*.

But if they live on a nonreligious *kibbutz*, how do they celebrate this occasion? At one time many of these *kibbutzim* used to ignore Jewish religious ceremonies altogether. But in recent years they, too, have come to the realization that a life without celebration, without itual and ceremony, is barren and empty, lacking one of the most important elements of identification with our people. Therefore they, too, have now begun to develop their celebration of Jewish rituals such as the Bar Mitzvah.

As a symbol of the acceptance of new responsibility on the part of the Bar Mitzvah boy, beginning at the age of twelve through his Bar Mitzvah, he is assigned thirteen special tasks. Each one of these tasks or goals are intended to teach him a greater sense of responsibility to the values that are important to the *kibbutz* and to the Jewish people.

For example, one of his assigned tasks is to stand guard for a night at a strategic place in the *kibbutz*. This has unhappily become a critically important responsibility in every *kibbutz* in Israel today.

Another task that he is given is to spend twenty-four hours alone, about a mile or so from the *kibbutz*, fending for himself, finding food, shelter, and the other basic necessities of survival.

In addition, there are also collective goals which are established for him and other twelve-year-olds. For example, in one *kibbutz* the kindergarten needed painting, so the entire group of Bar Mitzvah boys and Bat Mitzvah girls painted the kindergarten. Sometimes the youngsters choose to plant melons or other fruits. Then they sell them and contribute the proceeds to the funds for families of fallen soldiers or to some other worthwhile cause in order to practice the Jewish precept of *tzedakah*.

Other requirements are to study the history of their *kibbutz* and the history of the establishment of the State of Israel. Another requirement in many *kibbutzim* is to spend a day at a nearby friendly Arab village, trying to understand better the customs and life-styles of the Arab youngsters in order to help these young Israelis to learn how to live one day, hopefully, at peace with all of their Arab neighbors.

If the Bar Mitzvah boy has grandparents on the *kibbutz*, another task which is assigned to him is that every *Erev Shabbat*, for the entire year, he brings to the house of his grandparents either flowers or *challah* or some other gift in order to teach him the importance of cultivating love and respect for the older members of the family.

On many *kibbutzim* the children live separately from their parents, but during the Bar Mitzvah year it is expected that the Bar Mitzvah boy will spend more time with his parents, speaking to them about their past and learning more about their youth. He makes notes of these conversations and he also collects family pictures from his parents and creates a special family album in honor of his Bar Mitzvah.

On the day of his Bar Mitzvah (the day which is chosen is often *Lag B'omer*, which commemorates the heroism of Bar Kochba, who led the revolt of our people against the Romans in the second century), the ceremony usually consists of two parts. First, there is a reading from some part of the Torah, perhaps the Torah portion of that week or some other Torah portion which the boy chooses, and the Haftorah of his choice. A number of additional biblical texts and poetic selections from Israeli and other poets are then read by the boy, his parents, brothers, sisters, and friends.

The second part of the ceremony usually consists of some dramatic presentations by the Bar Mitzvah and his family. One of the favorite readings that the Bar Mitzvah boys on the *kibbutz* like to choose, because of its particular relevance to their situation in Israel today, comes from the thirty-fifth chapter of the prophet Isaiah:

## Living Courageously

*Ufduyey hashem yeshuvun uvaoo tzion b'rinah:*
"And the redeemed of the Lord shall return and come with singing unto Zion. They shall obtain gladness and joy and sorrow and sighing shall flee away."

After the ceremony come the gifts. First, the *kibbutz* presents the youngsters with a *Tanach*, a Bible, and also a wristwatch. Some *kibbutzim* also give him a gun or a rifle. To the Bar Mitzvah boy, the *kibbutz* gives a hoe; to the Bat Mitzvah girl a pruning fork—both symbols of responsibility for protecting the *kibbutz* and sharing in its work. In addition, each celebrant is presented with a book which reflects his own particular interest in literature. Then all of the assembled *kibbutz* members and invited guests join in a festive meal. They sing and dance together, rejoicing in the *simcha* of the newest Bar Mitzvah or Bat Mitzvah of the *kibbutz*.

Please note how closely these nonreligious *kibbutzim* approximate the religious tradition of celebrating a Bar Mitzvah, even though, I suspect, they would likely be the last ones ot admit it. But, in addition, they have added some very beautiful and wise goals or tasks, leading toward a greater sense of responsibility on the part of the Bar Mitzvah, from which it might be possible for us to learn a great deal in our own preparations for a Bar Mitzvah or Bat Mitzvah.

Let me now tell you about another kind of Bar Mitzvah. Brian Mizrach was born in San Francisco and grew up in that city. In 1972 his parents decided to take the family on a visit to Australia and from there to Israel. When they came to Israel, they fell in love with the country and decided to settle there. Last June, when the time for Brian's Bar Mitzvah arrived, a huge number of invitations were sent from his home in Herzliah to the many relatives, friends, and business acquaintances of his parents all over the world. But the invitation was very different from the usual one. This is how it read:

> At Brian's request, please no gifts. Instead, if you wish, please help us to plant the Brian Mizrach Grove by purchasing trees to be planted in Israel by the Jewish National Fund.

Brian Mizrach received more than one thousand gifts, none for himself. Instead, all the gifts were tree certificates for the trees that were to be planted in his Grove. In June, Brian, his family, and friends dedicated the Grove and planted the first trees in an area near the town of Modin. (Modin was the place where the Maccabees began their successful revolt against the Syrians, which we commemorate on the Festival of Hanukkah.) The next day Brian celebrated his Bar Mitzvah in the Synagogue in Herzliah, the city of his new home in the land of his ancient forefathers. Afterward his father commented: "Every year on Brian's birthday, we will go to Modin to visit Brian's Grove and see if the trees are keeping pace with Brian, as he grows into manhood and the trees grow into maturity."

What a marvelous way to celebrate a Bar Mitzvah! Not by teaching our children how much they should expect from others but rather by adding beauty and strength to the Promised Land of the Jewish people.

Finally, I would like to tell you about a third unusual Bar Mitzvah. This was described in an article in *The Village Voice* and was written by the noted jazz critic and writer Nat Hentoff. Nat Hentoff has, for a long time, been estranged from Jewish religious practices. As a matter of fact, in an essay which he wrote for *Commentary* in 1961, in a symposium for young, Jewish intellectuals, he said he hoped that "my children would have no need for any religion, Judaism included." But the Lord works in strange and wonderful ways, and Hentoff had failed to reckon with his stubborn, headstrong son, Nicholas. I would like to let you hear Nat Hentoff tell you the story himself. About Nicholas he writes:

> One direction I had never expected Nicholas to take was the route which led him, drawing his resistant parents along, to the Brotherhood Synagogue then on West 13th Street. The prospect of Nicholas as a Bar Mitzvah boy was at first beyond his parents' imagination because religion had no place in our home while he was growing up. We do have a Christmas tree every year, but since the pagans were on to that way of cheering up the long winter before Christians picked up the custom, I do not regard this annual enlivening of our living room as tribute to any spiritual overlord recognized in New York City!
>
> It's a long apology. So what did bring Nicholas to the Torah? I do occasionally use Yiddish words at home but by way of expletive rather than example. And there has always been our families—grandparents, aunts, uncles—at our annual Passover Seder. Those one-nighters, however, are much more like a camp reunion than a religious experience, having a rather manic ambi-

ance that, for one example, the speed with which the Haggadah is traversed in song and story decidedly accelerates each year!

Nick has also heard my tales of growing up Jewish in Boston during the years in which a Sunday radio sermon by Father Charles Coughlin, running the charges on the protocols of the elders of Zion, often resulted in cadres of his younger true believers cracking heads in Jewish neighborhoods like mine in the evenings that followed.

This much there was of a fractured Jewish background in Nick's life, but what actually specifically determined him to become an official Jew were two entertainments that kept reverberating in his head.

First, my wife and I took Nick and his younger brother Tom to a Saturday matinee performance of "The Rothschilds," and later we saw the film version of "Fiddler On The Roof." It was soon after Tevya had joined the Rothschilds in Nick's historical consciousness that he began to insist—insisting is his common level of discourse, he never merely asks—on having a Bar Mitzvah. My wife and I paid him little mind. It was, we thought, a transient enthusiasm like the coins and the baseball cards. Months went by and Nicholas continued to plan for his Bar Mitzvah. Eventually he wore us down and so we became members of the Brotherhood Synagogue and enrolled Nicholas in its Hebrew School. My wife and I still did not believe however that Nicholas, with all of his urgent avocations, would continue to be serious to the point of actually going through the special after-school preparations for a Bar Mitzvah. Yet on he plowed until one day in May of this year, I found myself buying Nick a Bar Mitzvah Tallit and the required white-lined yarmulke.

Continuing myself to be of little faith in the sustenance of faith, I borrowed a Tallit for the occasion from my father-in-law's brother-in-law—that's as far away as you can get!

Then he described Nick's preparation in the Synagogue, his studies, the difficulties he had with his teacher and with the Cantor, but nonetheless he persisted. And then came the great day of the Bar Mitzvah itself. Nicholas chanted the *Haftorah* and the blessings, and then he gave a little speech, in which he said:

> When I was a small child, I didn't really know the history behind my religion or the hardships my ancestors had to face. But as I started to grow older, I slowly began to grasp the real idea behind our religion. Then about three years ago, my parents took

me to two shows—Fiddler On The Roof and The Rothschilds—that opened my eyes to the fact that the Jewish people had not always had the joy I always thought was built into our religion.

Nat Hentoff writes: " 'Where and how did you ever get any idea,' I wondered, 'aside from those Marx Brothers Seders, of your religion before we took you to those shows?' "

Nick continued:

The Jewish people have been badly treated in most cultures. Even in the United States, when some of the earlier Jewish immigrants got off the boat, they were treated like cattle. If the immigration officials couldn't pronounce their names, the inspectors would just brand them with a new name. The Jewish immigrants often lived in slums surrounded by people who did not like having them there.

When my father was a child living in a Jewish neighborhood, the Jewish kids were often preyed on by groups of Italian and Irish kids. Once my father had to say that he was a Greek or he would have gotten beat up. I think it is horrible that a boy who is proud of his religion should have to deny his religion under the threat of getting beaten up.

Nat Hentoff interpolates: ". . . I told you that story, Nick, but did you have to repeat it in front of all these people? I had, it's true, written about the time I became an instant Greek but writing about it is one thing, trying in public to compose the proper facial expression of being appreciably memorialized as a coward is quite another!"

" 'I will close my speech,' Nick looked at the congregation, 'by saying something that is very sincere and comes from the bottom of my heart. I am very proud and glad to belong to the Jewish religion.' "

And then Nat Hentoff concluded:

A few days before the Bar Mitzvah, since I had a lot of catching up to do, I had been reading Benjamin Kaplan's "The Jew and His Family." In a section on the Jewish child in the Shtetl, in the small towns of eastern Europe in which Jews of the Diaspora lived, Kaplan noted that the Jewish child in the Shtetl was considered more than the mere result of the union of his parents, more than the sum of his ancestors. He contained another element for he had been touched by the finger of God. It was believed further that he transmitted Judaism generation after generation.

I don't know anything about God but thirty-six years after my own Bar Mitzvah I suddenly felt, not having worried about it before, that I had not let down my father and all the Hentoffs before him. My son had kept our Judaism alive. I myself had had very little to do with transmitting Judaism to Nick, but still one way or another, I had been a carrier.

That afternoon, after the guests had gone, Nick announced that he was going to continue to go to Hebrew School. After he had gone on his own this far, who would stop him? Anyway, being Nick, who could stop him?

In some very strange and mysterious way, the alienation of a Jewish father was transformed into the affirmation of a Jewish son, and therefore the link has not been permanently severed between the faith of our fathers and the future of a boy by the name of Nicholas Hentoff.

Each one of these Bar Mitzvahs is quite different and yet each one represents a special attempt to make this moment as beautiful and meaningful a Jewish experience as possible, an affirmation of a Tradition of four thousand years, a determination to live by the same faith for which our people lived and died in order to be Jews.

# 8.
# Kindling the Spark

What was the miracle of Hanukkah? One answer is found in the Book of Maccabees in the Apocrypha, which tells of the heroism of Mattathias and his sons, who possessed great faith in God and an intense love for Judaism. As a result, they were able to win a great victory over the stronger Syrian army.

But the Talmud provides a different answer to the question: What was the miracle of Hanukkah?

It tells the familiar story about Judah and his brothers, who, having liberated the Temple from the Syrians, discovered that all the oil had been defiled by the enemy. They were only able to find one little cruse of oil which had been hidden away and was still pure. With that oil they kindled the Menorah, which should have lasted for only one day. Instead, there was a miracle and the oil lasted for eight days.

On a symbolic level the story in the Talmud says something about each one of us, about every Jew. At times we Jews stray very far from our Jewishness. We incorporate so many of the values and the practices of the society which surrounds us that our Jewishness becomes almost unrecognizable. And yet, hidden away like that little cruse of oil, there is within the deepest recesses of every Jew a little spark. In Yiddish it is called *Dos pintele Yid*, a little spark of Jewishness which cannot be extinguished, and that, too, is a kind of miracle.

Let me give you some examples.

Theodor Herzl was a thoroughly assimilated Jew until he witnessed the Dreyfus trial where he saw the shameful degradation of an innocent man and the violent anti-Semitism of the supposedly liberal French people. Two years before, in December 1895, he was outraged by a statement made by the Chief Rabbi of Vienna, Rabbi Moritz Gudemann. Rabbi Gudemann had declared that the use of a Christmas tree in a Jewish home was un-Jewish. Herzl's own parents always had a Christmas tree in their home, which they called a "Hanukkah tree," and Herzl considered the Rabbi a benighted fanatic. Two years later, after the Dreyfus trial, Herzl wrote an obviously autobiographical story of how he celebrated Hanukkah once again and how the Menorah affected him and his children:

> Hitherto he had permitted to pass by unobserved the holiday which the wonderful apparition of the Maccabees had illumined for thousands of years with the glow of miniature lights. Now, however, he made this holiday an opportunity to prepare something beautiful which should be forever commemorated in the minds of his children. In their young souls should be implanted early a steadfast devotion to their ancient people. He bought a Menorah, and when he held this nine-branched candlestick in his hands for the first time, a strange mood came over him. In his father's house also, the lights had once burned in his youth, now far away, and the recollection gave him a sad and tender feeling for home. The tradition was neither cold nor dead—thus, it had passed through the ages, one light kindling another. The mere sound of the name, Menorah, which he now pronounced every evening to his children, gave him great pleasure. There was a lovable ring to the word when it came from the lips of little children.
> On the first night the candle was lit and the origin of the holiday explained. The wonderful incident of the lights that strangely remained burning so long, the story of the return from the Babylonian exile, the second Temple, the Maccabees—our friend told his children all he knew. It was not very much, to be sure, but it served. When the second candle was lit, they repeated what he had told them, and though it had all been learned from him, it seemed to him quite new and beautiful.
> When he had resolved to return to his people and to make open acknowledgement of his return, he had only thought he would be doing the honorable and rational thing. But he had never dreamed that he would find in it a gratification of his yearning for the beautiful. Yet nothing less was his good fortune. The Menorah with its many lights became a thing of beauty to inspire lofty thought.
> Then came the eighth day, when the whole row burns, even the faithful ninth, the servant, which on other nights is used only for the lighting of the others. A great splendor streamed from the Menorah. The children's eyes glistened. But for our friend all this was the symbol of the enkindling of a nation. When there is but

one light, all is still dark, and the solitary light looks melancholy. Soon it finds one companion, then another, and another. The darkness must retreat. When all the candles burn, then we must all stand and rejoice over the achievements. And no office can be more blessed than that of a Servant of the Light.

The miracle of Theodor Herzl, who helped to create the Jewish State, is the fact that the spark of his Jewishness had never been fully extinguished.

Let me tell you about another Jew who strayed very far from his Jewishness.

Supreme Court Justice Felix Frankfurter was one of the most distinguished and gifted judges to grace that Court. There was a period in his life when, under the inspiration of Louis Brandeis, Frankfurter became very active in the Zionist cause. In his later years, however, his association with Jewish life was virtually nonexistent. As for the Jewish religion, he had dismissed it from serious concern early in his life like so many other Jewish intellectuals of his generation.

Garson Kanin, in his book of reminiscences about Justice Frankfurter, writes that Mrs. Frankfurter became very concerned about her husband's preoccupation with his own funeral. One day, she said to Kanin:

> In all our years, I have never known him to give so much as a fleeting thought to the subject and now he simply won't get off it. Where. And how. And who . . . One of the many things that seem to worry him is the religious aspect. He is afraid that somehow there will be prayers or words spoken by a rabbi. He says he wants no such meaningless hypocrisy; that right or wrong, for better or for worse, he left the synagogue when he was fifteen and has never returned. He recalls that he sat there one morning, looked about him, and realized that the rituals and prayers meant a great deal to the others and nothing to him . . . so he left and never returned. He knows exactly the sort of ceremony he wants and above all, no prayers.

One day, as Mr. Kanin was leaving the ailing Justice, Mr. Frankfurter asked to see him privately. The subject—his funeral. He outlined the service and instructed Mr. Kanin: "I want you to see to it that none of my instructions are violated." Then he told him who the speakers should be.

"Finally," Mr. Kanin reports, "he names the last of the speakers."
"Do you know why I want *him?*" Frankfurter asks.
"No."
"Because he is my only close personal friend who is also a practicing, orthodox Jew. He knows Hebrew perfectly and will know exactly what to say." Remembering Mrs. Frankfurter's account, Mr. Kanin was astounded and asked: "Do you mean a prayer of some sort?"
"Well, of course, you nut, what else would he say in Hebrew."
"Then you do mean the Kaddish?"
"Oh, I don't know, and neither do you, but he'll know and he'll do it beautifully. Let me explain. I came into the world a Jew, I think it is fitting that I should leave as a Jew. I don't want to be one of these pretenders and turn my back on a great and noble heritage . . ."

*Dos pintele Yid,* seemingly lost for so many years, reappears as Frankfuter contemplates the end of his life.

Let me tell you about another person, in a story related by an Israeli journalist. The journalist has a friend who lives in Haifa who insisted that he join him in a visit to a monk of his acquaintance who was living in a monastery on Mount Carmel. His friend assured the writer that the visit would provide him with excellent material for a story. When they knocked at the door of the monastery, it was opened by an elderly monk who welcomed them warmly and led them to his room. The man was dressed in the garb characteristic of the Carmelite Order. The room was very austere in its furnishings, but the walls were adorned with many beautiful paintings. The visitors commented on the artistic merit of the paintings and asked the monk how he acquired so many fine works of art. Modestly he informed them that they were his own creations. They then asked him about his background, about his life before he had become a monk. Quietly he began to tell them his life's story. He was born in 1890, an only child of a prosperous Jewish merchant in a Russian Jewish community. His name was Isaac Galowitch. Already as a young child, his precocious artistic gifts became well known in the community. Eventually his reputation came to the attention of a rich rural squire by the name of Shakarmant. Prompted by envy or some other motive, the squire managed to have the child kidnapped and kept him hidden in his castle. The heartbroken parents and the police searched for the child but after a long time gave up the search.

When things had quieted down, Shakarmant took the boy to Moscow, had him baptized in the Russian church, and arranged for him to be raised as a Christian. As the boy grew into young manhood, he was sent to a Seminary. Ultimately, he was consecrated as a monk of the Carmelite Order and was assigned to this monastery in Israel, where he has been living for many years. In his leisure hours, surrounded by the breathtaking view from Mount Carmel, he has painted thousands of paintings, a few of which he has kept for his own room. The rest he presented as gifts to Russian churches throughout the world. In some of his paintings he has tried to recapture on canvas his memories of his childhood, the indistinct images of his father and mother. He has lost hope long ago of ever meeting any member of his Jewish family and is, therefore, all alone in the world. But he regards the land of Israel as his home and the people of Israel as his family.

Once a year on *Yom Kippur*, he comes to a synagogue in Haifa, seats himself inconspicuously in the rear of the Synagogue, and *davens* together with the congregation, weeping and pouring out his heart to God.

The spirit of *Yiddishkeit* cannot be extinguished and continues to live in the soul of this tragic human being.

What are the lessons we can derive from this remarkable truth about our people?

First, it is important to realize that every Jew we meet, however estranged he may be from our people, retains a spark of Jewishness within him, and it is up to us to help kindle that spark.

How do we do this? We never do it by discouraging him, or by making fun of his lack of knowledge, or by laughing at his unfamiliarity with Jewish practices. We can kindle that remarkable spark by bringing him closer to us, by inviting him to our home to celebrate Hanukkah or *Shabbat* or *Pesach*, by welcoming him to our Temple and making certain that he feels at home in our midst.

How did Hillel put it?

*Ohev et habriot umkorvan latorah:*
"Love your fellow man and thereby bring him closer to the Torah."

But there is yet another lesson in this mysterious spark within us. It says that each one of us, even those of us who are working hard at being Jewish, has within us additional sparks that await kindling. There are always more *Mitzvot* that we can perform. We can evidence greater concern for fellow Jews by greater generosity and greater involvement. We can become more ethical and more sensitive in our dealings with each other. No Jew is ever a completed Jew. Each one of us is always in the process, hopefully, of becoming a better Jew.

When we light the Menorah with our families on Hanukkah, let us recall the great miracle of Hanukkah, of that one hidden cruse of oil that remained pure. And let us create a new miracle for ourselves, of becoming the kind of Jews who are totally committed to our people and our Torah.

# 9.
# Hanukkah's Message Year Round

We love Hanukkah for the beauty of its lights, the *latkes* and jelly doughnuts, the *dreidel*, the gifts, and the fun. But even more, we sense that underneath the lights, the food, and the fun, there is a profound symbolism which speaks to us about the method and meaning of being Jewish year round.

For example, who is supposed to kindle the Hanukkah Menorah? Jewish Law is very specific: *"Hakol chayavim b'neyr Chanukkah, anashim, v'nashim, v'katan"*—All are responsible for lighting the Menorah, every man, woman and child. . . . To perform the *mitzvah* fully, every member of the family should participate.

If we are to strengthen our families, our Tradition says, we need to seek out opportunities to share together the experience of being Jewish. On Hanukkah, we light the Menorah together. On Purim, we come to the Synagogue together to listen to the *Megillah*. On Passover, we celebrate the Seder as a family.

Indeed, the Jewish family needs strengthening. Dr. Alvin Schiff, Executive Vice President of the Board of Jewish Education of Greater New York, on the basis of recent studies, made the following predictions about the Jewish family in the eighties. He projected that (1) One out of two Jews who marry in the 1980s will be divorced by 1990. (2) One out of two Jewish college students who marry in the 1980s will marry out of the Jewish faith. (3) One out of every two Jewish families will not be affiliated with a synagogue or with any Jewish organization. (4) Two out of every five Jewish children will receive no Jewish education and will not celebrate a Bar or Bat Mitzvah. (5) Approximately 40 percent of the young adults involved in missionary and cult groups will be Jewish by birth.

There are Jewish parents who take their children to see the Celtics and the Patriots. There are some who coach their children in Little League. There are parents who will not miss their children's soccer games. There are others who take their children to museums and concerts and movies. All of these can be excellent experiences. From their parents' enthusiasm, these children learn to love athletics, music, and culture. But if we are to flourish as Jews, we need Jewish parents who are equally passionate about taking their children to Services every *Shabbat*, who are equally serious about teaching by example the sacredness of prayer each day, who are equally concerned that their children should see them giving *tzedakah* regularly.

The late Dr. Abraham Joshua Heschel once said at a White House Conference, "Unless a fellowship of spiritual experience is re-established, the parents will remain outsiders to the child's soul. Friendship, affection is not acquired by giving presents. Friendship, affection comes about by two people sharing a significant moment, by having an experience in common."

"All are responsible for lighting the Menorah." If we want our families to be Jewish, we must constantly seek out and share those "significant Jewish moments" that our Tradition provides for us not only on Hanukkah but each day of the year.

When are you supposed to kindle the Menorah? You should light the candles as soon as the first stars appear in the sky. But if you are delayed, you may kindle the Menorah all night as long as the family is still awake. But what happens if you come home so late that the family is already asleep? Then, the Law says, *"Madlik v'ayno mevarech"*—You may kindle the lights but without a blessing.

The *Halacha* is saying to us, "Everybody has to be awake to the importance of this great *mitzvah*; otherwise, the blessing is missing." If the family is not there to see the kindling, the impact of the *mitzvah* has disappeared. Each of us is constantly given the opportunity to do *mitzvot* in our lives, but we have to be awake and alert to the possibilities which come our way.

I am certain that you shared my pride in a young woman from Newton, Pamela Glaser, whose story appeared in the media nationwide. Pamela is the top-ranked U.S. woman athlete in amateur karate. She learned in July that the tryouts for this year's World Karate Championship would take place on *Rosh Hashanah*. She tried, by writing many letters, to get the Committee to change the date, which they refused to do. She finally went to court and, ultimately,

U.S. District Judge Rya Zobel ordered that she be made a full member of the United States team, even though she missed the tryouts.

Pamela said that her decision to forgo the tryouts, which might have meant that she would not be on the team, was a very difficult one. She said, "I cried through half of the *Rosh Hashanah* Service." But she also added, "Religion is very important to me. It's very important that I stand up and say that I'm Jewish and proud of it."

Pamela could easily have rationalized her participating in the tryouts. She could have said, "Well, this once, I will forgo my observance of *Rosh Hashanah* and do the tryout. In the future, they probably won't be held on *Rosh Hashanah* anyhow." Instead, when the conflict arose, she was awake and alert to the *mitzvah* before her. It was not only the *mitzvah* of observing the holiness of *Rosh Hashanah*, which she refused to violate. In addition, she performed one of the greatest of all *mitzvot*, the *mitzvah* of *Kiddush Hashem*, the sanctification of God's name, by proclaiming to the Karate Committee and to the world, "I am a Jew; I am proud of my heritage, and like the Maccabees, I will not permit anybody to deprive me of my religious convictions."

Because Pamela Glaser was awake to the *mitzvah* of affirming her Jewishness, she has become a blessing not only to herself but to every Jew.

Finally, let me share with you a beautiful *minhag*, a Hanukkah custom practiced by Sefardic Jews in Jerusalem. They arrange for festive meals to be held on Hanukkah, and these meals have a special purpose. Listen to their description: *"Vechol mi shenafal riv bayno uvayn chaveyro mitpaysim b'soodot ayleh"*—Whoever has had a fight with another person during the year invites the other to these festive meals and establishes peace with one another.

What a wonderful custom for all of us to adopt. Imagine what that could mean to our families and our relationships. What wonders it could accomplish for the brothers and sisters who no longer speak to one another, for the parents and children who are estranged from each other, for good friends who have become bitter enemies. Imagine how much bitterness, rancor, and heartbreak we could eliminate from our hearts and souls, those cancerous feelings that destroy so many of the joys and pleasures of human life.

Recently, I had the privilege of being present at such a reconciliation in a family, and I share this experience with you with their permission. I came to visit an ill person at his home. His wife asked me to wait before I entered his room because he was in the midst of an extraordinary phone conversation. When the phone conversation was over, I entered his room and he told me this story. He had grown up with the companionship of a cousin whom he loved very much. But a rift developed in the family. Brothers and sisters stopped talking to each other and he was forbidden to see his beloved cousin. During his illness, a mutual friend mentioned to his cousin that he had been ill for a long time. She thereupon wrote him a beautiful letter, wishing him a speedy recovery and asking him if, despite their parents' estrangement, it was not finally time for them to speak to each other again. He was deeply moved by her letter and decided to call her so as to reestablish a relationship that had been broken many years before. They both wept as they spoke. They cried from the joy of rediscovering one another. He then invited her and her family to spend Thanksgiving with him and his family. Their children met each other for the first time on Thanksgiving. Two families have rediscovered each other and now share the happiness that comes with reconciliation and love.

Do you see why Sefardic Jews hold such meals on Hanukkah? Because on Hanukkah we commemorate the miracle of the Maccabees and the oil and it is appropriate that on Hannukah we should create a new miracle each year. It is the miracle of people who are able to sweep away the accumulated cobwebs of bitterness and anger, who can teach themselves and their children the strength of the spirit and exultation of the soul which come with an act of forgiveness.

When Hanukkah leaves us for another year, we need its teachings for the rest of the year. We need to create more opportunities for sharing "sacred Jewish moments" with our children to make them want to be Jews. We need to be awake to the *mitzvot* which beckon to us each day of the year. We need to cultivate the art of forgiveness so that the bonds between us that were severed in anger may be restored in friendship and love.

# 10.
# Falling in Love With Torah

We are approaching *Simchat Torah* and I want to discuss with you the significance of its symbols.

The whole day, of course, centers about the Torah. The Rabbis see the Torah as the *kallah*, the bride. Concluding the reading of the Torah, the *Chag Hasiyum* is the wedding. The Jewish people are the *Hatan*, the groom. The person who is called to the Torah as we conclude its reading, the *Hatan Torah*, is the bridegroom of the Torah representing all of us. The one who is called to the Torah as we begin its reading once again, the *Hatan Breshit*, is the bridegroom of the beginning, again representing us all.

In some communities in Europe, during the late Middle Ages, the wife of the *Hatan Torah* was called *Kallat Torah*, the bride of the Torah. And the wife of the *Hatan Breshit* was called *Kallat Breshit*.

What does all this symbolism mean? If a Jew is ever to fully understand the beauty of being a Jew, it says that somewhere along the way he simply has to fall in love with the Torah and with Judaism. Some people have a fleeting acquaintance with Torah; some respect it but don't really know it well; some never even give themselves a chance to get to know it.

How do you get to love the Torah? First, by getting to know it well. You have to study the Bible and learn about our great heroic figures who were also very human. You have to listen to the message of the Prophets who insisted on justice for the oppressed. You have to be willing to enter the world of the Talmud and experience the intellectual challenge of wrestling with some of the greatest minds that ever lived, as they attempted to apply the teachings of Torah to every moment of a person's life. You have to familiarize yourself with the poets, philosophers, and teachers of the Middle Ages and of modern times, who struggled with the perennial problems that beset human beings: the dilemmas of mortality, evil, and suffering. In order to develop a love for Torah, you have to study it and imbibe its profundity and its wisdom.

But study is not enough. To fall in love with Torah and Judaism you have to experience its beauty, warmth, and happiness. How does the Psalmist put it?

> *Taamu ur'u ki tov hashem:*
> "*Taste* and see the goodness of the Lord."

You have to experience the taste, the flavor, the *taam* of being a Jew in order to fall in love with it. You have to observe *Shabbat* together with your family by going to the Synagogue, by observing it in your home with its beautiful rituals, by singing *zmirot*, and by enjoying each other's presence.

You have to celebrate *Sukkot* by building a *sukkah* with your children, decorating it, and eating in it. You have to enjoy the pleasure of being in the Synagogue, walking in a circuit with the *etrog* and *lulav*. You have to join in singing the beautiful *Hallel* prayers and shake the *etrog* and *lulav* in every direction, thanking God for His blessings, which come from every direction.

You have to celebrate *Simchat Torah* by singing and dancing with the Torah, by circling the Synagogue in the *Hakafot,* by watching your children march with their flags and their apples.

Those are some of the experiences of being a Jew. The Torah provides us with such experiences each day of our lives.

Our rabbinic sources tell us of yet another symbol on *Simchat Torah*:

> *Nohagim l'ateyr et sifrey hatorah biktarim shelahem:*
> "It is customary to place crowns upon the Torahs."

This means that a Jew ought to place the values of Torah and Judaism above all other values.

We acquire our values from many sources, often the worst sources.

During adolescence, when we desperately wish to be part of the peer group, we usually see our peers experimenting with drugs, alcohol, and shoplifting (a popular suburban sport). We acquire values from watching TV, from reading magazines and newspapers. What do we derive from these media? We are inundated by countless programs of violence and killing. We are treated to the suicidal delights of Eval Knevil. We are overwhelmed by the prurient offerings of pornography. I had a boy in one of my classes who challenged my views regularly. He was forever quoting to me from *Penthouse* magazine, the "new revelation" from Sinai.

A Jew who falls in love with Torah makes the values of Torah his values, goals, and ideals. A value such as *v'nishmartem m'od l'nafshoteychem* says that a Jew must never do anything to harm his health, whether by smoking, drugs, or excessive alcohol.

*Lo tignov*, the eighth commandment, tells us that theft is forbidden, whether it is collusion among industrial giants or even stealing a twenty-five-cent item from a drugstore.

Another Jewish value is *tzniut*, modesty. It says that regardless of the latest fad, whether it be streaking, or nude swimming, and regardless of what *Penthouse* preaches, a Jew is supposed to be modest, to respect the dignity of the image of God in which he has been created.

The conflict of values of our society with the values of the Torah was best expressed by the Rabbis in the form of a parable. Those who have no permanent values may be likened to a man who is standing in total darkness. When he starts to walk, he stumbles over a stone and falls. He continues on his way, comes to a ditch, falls in, and hurts himself. Why? Because he has no lamp in his hand to light his path.

But those who live by the teachings of the Torah can be compared to a person who is standing in darkness but who has a lamp in his hand. He walks and sees a stone but does not stumble over it. He sees a ditch but avoids it because he has the lamp of the Torah in his hand.

The Psalmist expressed it this way:

> Thy word is a lamp unto my feet,
> And a light unto my path.

There is one more beautiful symbol associated with *Simchat Torah*. The Rabbis say:

> *Od nahagu likrot kol han'arim l'sefer torah:*
> "It is customary to call all the children to the Torah."

The Torah has a future and the Jewish people has a future only if there are children who can be called to the Torah, who study Torah, who fall in love with Torah. Even the enemies of our people understood this secret of Jewish survival. The Midrash says that the nations of the world came to consult with their wisest men, Balaam ben Beor, the biblical soothsayer, and Avnimos, the Gentile philosopher. They asked these men this question: "How can we finally destroy the Jewish people?" Whereupon these wise men replied:

*Lechu v'chizru al batey k'neysiot v'al batey midrashot shelahen:*
"Go to their Synagogues and schools."

*v'im m'tzatem sham tinokot metzaftzefin b'kolan eyn atem yecholim l'hizdaveg lahem:*
"And if you find children there studying Torah, you will never be able to destroy them."

Even when the Jewish condition was most grim, we Jews never ceased to study Torah, to teach it to our children, and to celebrate *Simchat Torah*.

Elie Wiesel once told this story about an incident that took place in one of the concentration camps in the shadow of the death chambers. In one of the barracks, several hundred Jews gathered to celebrate *Simchat Torah*. They wanted to have the *hakafot*, the procession with the Torah. But they had no Torah and were at a loss as to how to proceed. Suddenly, an old man noticed a young boy nearby and asked him, "Do you remember what you learned?" The boy answered, "Yes, I do." The old man asked, "Do you remember *Shema Yisrael?*" And the boy replied, "I remember much more." But the man said, *"Shema Yisrael* is enough." Whereupon he lifted the boy onto his shoulders and the boy sang *"Shema Yisrael,"* and the old man danced with the boy as though he were the Torah, and all the others sang and danced around the boy and cried.

We rejoice on *Simchat Torah* because we can bring Jewish children to the Torah.

# 11.
# The People of the Book

It was Mohammed who called us the "People of the Book." He recognized that our religion stems from a book called the Torah, and he saw the great love of our people for books and for literary creativity.

I do not know of any other people who have a festival devoted to rejoicing over a book, like our *Simchat Torah*. When a religious book falls, we lift it up and kiss it. Just as there is the great *mitzvah* of *Pidyon Shvuyim*, rescuing prisoners, so, too, is there a *mitzvah* of *Pidyon Sfarim*, rescuing the books stolen from Jewish communities by bandits, who knew that Jews would spend great amounts of money to redeem their books.

When a sacred book is no longer usable, we do not discard it, nor do we burn it. We bury it with the same honor we accord a human being.

In the twentieth century our greatest enemy, Adolf Hitler, continued the policies of the Inquisition and destroyed some eight million Jewish books. But suddenly there was a change in this policy. Instead of destroying Jewish books, he had them transported to secret destinations. After the war, we learned the meaning of this new policy. The Germans were convinced that they would be successful in their attempt at genocide. They decided that after all the Jews had been exterminated, there would be a need for a "Jewish Institute" where every Jewish book would be assembled. German scholars would then quote from these books (with their genius at distortion), to show the world why it was necessary to rid mankind of this detestable people. Though Hitler intended it otherwise, he helped save approximately half a million Jewish books, many of which are now part of the library of the Hebrew University in Jerusalem.

For the same reason, in Soviet Russia today, the government

permits no publishing of prayerbooks or any other Hebrew books, in the knowledge that if you deprive Jews of their books long enough, you may succeed in eliminating them as a people altogether. That is why Jewish visitors try to smuggle in Jewish prayerbooks, Bibles, and calendars to Russian Jews—these are the only sources of the Jewish book.

But no tyrant has ever succeeded in separating the Jew from his Torah. In his book, *Nitzotzey Gvurah,* "Sparks of Heroism," Moshe Prager tells the story of the Rabbi of Antwerp, Belgium, who was being led onto a death train by the Nazis. The Nazis had destroyed that once proud Jewish community, but the Rabbi managed to save two things: in one hand, he held a *Sefer Torah,* the last *Sefer Torah* of Antwerp. And in the other hand, he held a little boy whose parents had already been killed by the Nazis. And with those two treasures, the Rabbi walked into the train which took him to his death.

To the very end, a Jew could not be severed from his Torah or his child, both of whom represent his hope for the future.

Let me tell you one more story from the Holocaust which took place in the Hassag Labor Camp. The Jewish prisoners wanted to celebrate *Simchat Torah,* but how do you celebrate without a Torah? A Jewish cobbler who was permitted to come and go freely because he made boots for the officers, bribed a guard and promised to make him a pair of officer's boots. In return, the guard permitted him to take a small *Sefer Torah* which had been confiscated by the Nazis. The cobbler wrapped the Torah around his waist and smuggled it into the camp. The Jews concealed the Torah in the hollow under one of their wooden beds. On *Simchat Torah* night, they gathered in the barracks, danced around the barrack doing the *hakafot,* and each time they passed the wooden cot, they leaned over and kissed the board that lay directly above the Torah. They sang and danced in silence lest they be heard by the guards. They sang:

*Sisu v'simchu b'simchat torah ki hi lanu oz v'orah:*
"Rejoice and be happy on *Simchat Torah,* because the Torah is our strength and our light!"

This Torah was miraculously saved and is in the Synagogue of the Gerer Hasidim in B'nai Brak, Israel.

Perhaps the Jewish attitude toward the Torah was best exemplified eighteen centuries ago. During the Roman persecutions of our people in the second century, the Romans also understood the importance of Jewish books and forbade the observance of Judaism. They especially warned against any who would dare to teach the Torah to other Jews. Rabbi Hananiah ben Teradyon nonetheless persisted in teaching Torah publicly. He was arrested by the Romans while teaching his disciples from a *Sefer Torah*. They wrapped him in the Scroll of the Torah and burned him alive. His heartbroken disciples, seeking a last word of comfort, said to him:

*Rabi, ma atah roeh?:*
"Rabbi, what do you see?"

He replied:

*Gvilin nisrafin v'otiot porchot:*
"I see the parchment burning while the letters of the Torah soar heavenward."

Our people is alive today because our Torah and our books have continued to live. Regardless of how much our most precious treasures have been hurt and destroyed, Israel continues to live because each Jew knows that only the parchment of the Torah can be destroyed, but the Divine letters continue to live in our hearts and in our souls forever.

# 12.
# The Sabbath of Our Liberation

On *Shabbat Hagadol*, the Great Sabbath preceding Passover, I would like to discuss with you one of the great mysteries of the Passover story. How was Moses able to make the Israelites understand the meaning of freedom? After all, they had been slaves for four hundred years and never knew the experience of freedom. They never knew that they could be anything else but slaves.

The Midrash suggests an answer. It comments on the words:

*Vayar b'sivlotam:*
"Moses saw their burdens."

*Raah she'eyn lahem m'nuchah:*
"He saw that they had no rest."

*Halach v'amar l'pharo: im eyn atta meyniach lahem yom echad, heym meytim:*
"He went to Pharaoh and said, 'If you won't give these slaves one day off, they will surely die.'"

*Amar lo: leych v'asey lahem kmo sheatta omeyr:*
"Pharaoh replied: "Then do something about it.'"

*Halach Mosheh v'tikeyn lahem et hashabat lanuach:*
"Moses then arranged for the Israelites to begin to observe the Sabbath each week."

The Midrash suggests that Moses not only wanted the Israelites to have a day of rest, which they needed desperately. He also wanted them to have a very special kind of day, *Shabbat*, on which they would begin to understand for the first time the taste and meaning of freedom. He knew that once they would enjoy the freedom of *Shabbat*, they would be able to understand what he meant when he told them that God wanted them to be completely free from the cruelty and oppression of Pharaoh and his taskmasters.

The truth is that people may be enslaved in many ways, not only in the physical bondage of an Egypt, but people may even be enslaved in a free land, even if they do not realize it.

Some people are slaves to their work. Their job becomes their all-consuming passion, to the neglect of their families and friends. Some people are slaves to competition; they constantly strive for greater wealth, for enhanced status. Even students feel this competition. Some students are not satisfied even if they receive a good grade in an exam. It has to be better than the next person's otherwise they are dissatisfied. We can become enslaved to our work.

*Shabbat* is Judaism's answer to that problem. It says: On one day a week, stop your work, your struggle, your competition. Join your fellow Jews in the Synagogue, in prayer, friendship, and unity. Try to become at one with your fellow man, with God, and with the universe.

But people are enslaved in other ways, too. For some, work and competition are not the problem anymore. For some, there is the problem of too much leisure, of not knowing what to do with all their free time. Some are made slaves by their own leisure. Because they have too much leisure, some people are always bored. They have tried everything, and nothing interests or excites them. They turn to drugs to create some excitement, some lift, to give them a "high," even if, in the process, they may be destroying themselves.

There are some who find that leisure heightens their tension because they see no purpose in their lives. They don't feel needed and therefore they resort to tranquilizers to make them less tense, but still their problem remains unresolved.

Most people in our society are always tired, often from doing nothing. They wake up exhausted and use "pep" pills as the solution to the problem of their fatigue. We are enslaved by our leisure.

*Shabbat* is an answer to the problem of our leisure as well. On *Shabbat*, you can use leisure creatively through worship by thinking of God and what He requires of you. On *Shabbat*, you can study and deepen your understanding of the greatest of all books, the Torah. On *Shabbat*, you are supposed to spend time with your family, not in a car in traffic jams and on gas-polluted roads, but at home. You can take a walk with your family or friends and begin again to appreciate together the beauty of God's universe.

In addition, on *Shabbat* afternoon it is customary to take a nap, because when you observe the Sabbath, you can throw away your sleeping pills. *Shabbat* brings surcease and relaxation, and even the worst insomniac can fall asleep on *Shabbat!*

Finally, there are people who are enslaved because they have no values, standards, or guidelines for their lives. Therefore, they fall prey to every fad: astrology, the occult, Zen Buddhism (anything but Judaism!). They have no code of morality and therefore anything goes. For example, at first the universities introduced coed dormitories. Now, at the University of Michigan, a group of students have decided to have coeducational rooms in the interest of scientific experiment! When we have no values, we are also enslaved.

*Shabbat* is a reminder of one of the greatest of Jewish values. It says you can take a day which to the rest of the world may simply be Saturday but to Jews it is *Shabbat Kodesh*, a Day of Holiness. It is a day which reminds us that anything in life can be made holy. Our words become holy when they are used for purposes of friendship, for giving comfort and strength to others. Our deeds become holy when they are motivated by justice and compassion. Our food becomes holy when it is kosher and when the meal becomes an encounter with the Divine. Our sexual relationship becomes holy between a married couple who have made a lifelong commitment of love to each other.

The Talmud says:

> *Ilamaley m'shamrin b'ney yisrael shtey shabatot k'hilchatan,*
> *miyad nigalin:*
> "If the children of Israel would observe two Sabbaths completely, they would immediately be redeemed."

The Sabbath taught our ancestors in Egypt the meaning of freedom. If we would observe it in our own lives today, it could yet redeem us from our own self-imposed enslavements.

*Shabbat Hagadol*, the Great Sabbath, is so called because it precedes Passover. More importantly, this day can become *Shabbat Hagadol* for each of us who would want to begin the process of our own liberation. Each of us has the possibility of making each *Shabbat* of the future a *Shabbat Hagadol* in our own lives.

# 13.
# Entropy Versus Seder

When life seems to overwhelm you, when disorder seems to envelop you, when you feel that you are becoming the living embodiment of Murphy's law, "If anything can go wrong, invariably it will," it may be a small comfort for you to learn that you are the victim of what scientists call *entropy*.

In an insightful essay by science writer K. C. Cole, she points out that disorder is the natural order of things in the universe and that entropy is the precise measure of the amount of disorder.

Let me give you some examples of entropy. Children's rooms, if left alone, tend to become messy instead of neat. Wood, if uncared for, will rot, metal will rust, flowers will wither, and paint will peel. If you don't take care of a house, your roof will eventually begin to leak.

This writer suggests that we humans see entropy in many other places in our lives as well. We see it at work in marriages that are falling apart. We see it in our country, which is suffering from inflation, unemployment, and a lack of direction from Washington. We see entropy in the relationships between nations, with the growing fear shared by so many of the possibility of a nuclear war that will destroy us all. Entropy seems to be encroaching upon our lives; an avalanche of disorder seems ready to inundate us all.

It is clear that there is a need to do something to counteract all the entropy in our world lest all of us be overwhelmed. I would suggest that we need to cultivate the very opposite of entropy and disorder, which is *seder*, or order, symbolized by the Seder we celebrate on the first two nights of Passover.

To create a Seder, as all of us know, takes a great deal of energy and effort. It means cleaning the house thoroughly, changing the dishes, preparing the Passover foods, and studying the *Haggadah*. When you put all of that together, you create a soul-stirring, memorable pageant of freedom, family, and friendship.

The only way to combat entropy in our lives is by investing our energy not only in creating a *Seder shel Pesach*, a Seder on Passover, but a *seder hachayim*, an order and meaning to our own lives.

Take the entropy which is threatening so many marriages and causing so many divorces. To create a *seder hachayim*, husbands and wives have to work much harder to make marriage work. They must never take each other for granted, and they have to rearrange the priorities of their lives. The first priority must be that marriage is more important than career, status, and acquisition.

A man who was divorced and is now remarried, said to me recently, "I've learned from my first marriage that you have to pay attention to a wife." I told him he was right, and you have to do the same for a husband.

An editor of the *Washington Monthly*, Gregg Easterbrook, describes some friends of his, a man and woman who moved in together recently. Before moving in, they had already set a date as to when they would break up. Their reasons for breaking up? The woman planned to change jobs and move from the city but the man did not plan to follow her. An eventual split was unfortunate, they agreed, but it was also inevitable, so why not plan on it in advance? About which the writer comments: "More and more, people are ordering their lives along a principle I call the 'automatic out.' In love, friendship, work, and the community, people increasingly prefer arrangements that automatically end at some pre-set date. . . . 'Automatic-out' is a force in society as a whole, as more of us hunger for lives that appear stable and deep-rooted but lack the complications of commitment."

He sees the same phenomenon occurring not only among those who live together without marriage but even among those couples who get married. They seem to feel that if something isn't going to last anyhow, why do I have to sacrifice for my partner? The short-term benefits of marriage are still popular, such as companionship, warmth, and convenience. But a long-term obligation to marriage has fallen into disrepute among many people today. A lack of commitment to marriage and to a partner has to create entropy, the disorder and disintegration of marriage. In Jewish Tradition, marriage requires a *Mesader Kiddushin*, involving two people who create a relationship of holiness, a relationship which requires hard work, love, and lifelong commitment to each other.

These days, our country itself is also feeling the effects of entropy. The unemployment rate has just reached the highest figure since World War II: 9 percent for the general population, 18 percent for blacks, 46 percent for black teenagers; all told: 9½ million people. These are only statistics, but imagine the frightening possibilities of riots and disorders in a country where so many people feel they have no stake in society, with no job, no hope, and no future. They are only statistics, but behind each of those statistics is a person with a family and each one of the members of that family is profoundly affected by a job that is lost. Even before you are fired, a feeling of fear begins to pervade your company, often accompanied by depression, in what psychologists call "the pink slip syndrome."

And when the axe finally falls? Mental health clinics report a sharp rise in people seeking help for family disturbances and emotional problems. Dr. Paula Rayman, a sociologist at Brandeis University, who has been conducting in-depth interviews of laid-off workers for several years, finds that many marriages have deteriorated and many have been shattered as a result of someone being fired. In Los Angeles, Dr. Ralph Catalino reports that when unemployment goes up, there is a significant increase in child abuse. He says: "This is frightening, because social costs of this kind will not go away when the economy gets better. Those kids are likely to suffer from it for life, and we may be paying the costs of this recession 18 years from now, when they grow up."

In a study of the effects of unemployment in Michigan, it was found that the main emotional victim of a plant shutdown was often not the person who was fired but someone else in the family. It might be the unemployed man's wife, who has to worry about her husband's morale, cope with his anger, buy the family food and other essentials with less money, and often has to take a low-paying job she dislikes. Dr. Lewis Furman, director of the study, asks the painful question: "Who strokes the stroker?"

It is ironic and tragic that these people are turning in great numbers to mental health facilities, but because the government has eliminated its support from these facilities, they, in turn, are cutting down on their services to the people who need them most.

There is a growing entropy in our land today and one of the major reasons, I believe, is because we have a President who is lacking in *rachmanut*. He lacks compassion for those who are losing jobs, for those who are poor, for those who need food stamps to survive, for children who are unlucky enough to have been born into poor families.

We need a new *seder* in our country today, a *seder* in which people will once again hear the words with which every Passover Seder begins: *"Kol Dichfin Yetey V'yeychol"*—Let all who are hungry and all who are in need enter and we will extend a helping hand to you. We are a country and a nation who have always been known for our compassion and we must raise our voices in protest against a President and an administration that have compassion only for the wealthy, the powerful, and the influential.

There is not only entropy within our country today. There is also entropy in the relationships between the nations of the world, in particular between the two superpowers, the United States and Russia. That entropy evidences itself in the global climate of fear and suspicion and the constant fashioning of more terrible nuclear weapons and delivery systems by both of our nations.

Why is there suddenly so much concern about nuclear arms in our country and in the world? After all, we have had these weapons for many years. Our administration has helped to create that fear. When President Reagan and Secretary of State Haig began talking about the possibility of fighting and winning "limited nuclear wars," people all over the world became frightened and outraged. Without being experts, they know that nuclear war means total annihilation for all of us and they began to react against the insanity that was being preached in Washington by leaders of our country. That is why there is so much support in Congress, in our country, and in the world for a nuclear freeze by both superpowers. We want to live and we want our children to have a future, and we are afraid to entrust our lives and our destinies to those who speak of "limited nuclear wars." The people of this country and of the world are asking for a Seder, a *seder olam*, a peaceful and sane order to the universe. They want a Seder which will welcome the prophet Elijah, who will announce the beginning of a new era when people will hate war and destruction so much that they will together bring about a Messianic time when, in the words of Isaiah, *"Lo yisa goy el goy cherev v'lo yilmidu od milchamah"*—Nation shall not lift up sword against nation. Neither shall they learn war anymore.

# 14.
# The Importance of a Mitzvah

A person who becomes a Bar Mitzvah is now a "son of the commandments." From now on he is obligated to fulfill the commandments of Judaism. The word *mitzvah* means not only commandment but later on in our Tradition takes on the meaning of any act of goodness, even one not specifically prescribed by the Tradition.

Today I would like to discuss with you the concept of *mitzvah*, some of the teachings of the Bible and Talmud about this system of "action symbols" through which we sanctify our lives.

Ben Azzai in *Pirkey Avot* said:

*Mitzvah goreret mitzvah:*
"Fulfilling one *mitzvah* causes us to fulfill another *mitzvah*."

Ben Azzai says that it is important for a person to establish the right kind of habits, not only physical habits like brushing our teeth every morning but habits of performing the kind of acts which will train us in the pattern of righteous living. For instance, our grandmothers used to keep *pushkes* on the closet doors and drop coins of *tzedakah* into them before *Shabbat*. It was a way of saying that *Shabbat* can only be joyous if we help others at the same time.

Our Tradition inculcated the idea of giving *tzedakah* at every opportunity. On *Pesach* we begin the Seder with:

*Kol dichfin yetei v'yeychol:*
"Let all who are hungry come and join us at our Seder."

On Purim, one of the most important *mitzvot* is giving *matanot la'evyonim*—gifts to the needy.

On *Sukkot*, we not only eat our meals in the *sukkah* with our family but we invite a poor person to join us in the *sukkah*.

Our Tradition created constant opportunities for us to establish the habit of *tzedakah*, until it became an integral part of our lives.

Ben Azzai maintains that once you have experienced the joy that comes with performing a *mitzvah*, you will have created within yourself the desire to fulfill yet another *mitzvah*.

A non-Jewish woman questioned me recently about the wonderful work being done by a local Jewish organization. She had asked its members how they happened to get involved in such work, and their only explanation was, "It's a *mitzvah*." She wanted to understand the meaning of *mitzvah* and the strength of an idea which could impel people to do so much good.

There are different kinds of *mitzvot*. There are *mitzvot beyn adam lamakom*, the ritual commandments, and *mitzvot beyn adam lachavero*, the ethical commandments.

Our Tradition recognized the danger, especially with regard to the ritual commandments, of performing *mitzvot* mechanically, without feeling, thought, or meaning.

The prophet Isaiah, in God's name, castigates people who worship God in such a way:

> And the Lord said: Because this people draw near,
> and with their mouth and with their lips do honor
> Me, but have removed their hearts far from Me,
> vathi yiratam oti mitzvat anashim melumadah—
> Their reverence for Me is a *mitzvah* learned by rote.

In order to pray well, for example, there is need for study, and practice, and preparation to enable one to enter into the right kind of mood and spirit. The Rabbis point out the importance of *kavanah*, of inwardness and feeling, as indispensable requisites of prayer, not the quantity of our prayers or the speed with which we utter them.

A *mitzvah* must not be performed mechanically. Take the wonderful *mitzvah* of *kashrut*, which enables us to sanctify our homes as well as identify with our people. Unless *kashrut* is observed with feeling, unless its meaning is explained, unless it is surrounded by blessings and an atmosphere of reverence and beauty, it can become mechanical, lifeless, and burdensome.

A *mitzvah*, if it is to be performed correctly, demands from us an investment of thought, emotion, and meaningful action.

There is a beautiful proverb about the concept of *mitzvah* in the

Midrash which shows the brilliant insight of the Rabbis into what we now call psychosomatic medicine, the influence in illness of the mind upon the body and vice versa. The Midrash says: "The gate which is not open to *mitzvot* will be opened to the physician."

What the Rabbis are saying is that performing a *mitzvah* is not simply an act to be performed by *tzadikim*, by saints. They say that the performance of *mitzvot* is a basic requisite to living a healthy life. As human beings, we are faced with the choice of either emerging from our own petty concerns to the broader needs of humanity or to begin to shrink in spiritual stature. If we do not enlarge our horizons, we begin to turn increasingly inward with growing concern and fear for ourselves, our feelings, our needs, obsessed by an unhealthy and morbid preoccupation with the smallest incident that may happen to us.

I know a woman who has no children and who has grown increasingly inward with the passing years. Instead of getting a job or doing volunteer work for some charitable organization, she is forever at home, constantly suffering from imaginary aches and pains, running from one doctor to another. If you happen to ask her, "How are you?" she responds with a whole list of complaints that grows longer each day. I always have the feeling that if this woman would leave her house and perform a few *mitzvot*, she would be an altogether different person. "The gate which is not open to *mitzvot* will be opened to the physician."

The concept of *mitzvah* is one of the great ideas created by our Tradition. May we become the kind of people who will seek out every opportunity to perform a *mitzvah*. Each time we fulfill a *mitzvah*, it will be a reminder of a loving God who has given us these wonderful instruments in order to sanctify our lives and at the same time bring a measure of strength and comfort to our fellow man.

# 15.
# Total Involvement in a *Mitzvah*

On *Sukkot*, a Hasid was once not feeling well. Despite his wife's warning that he would catch a cold if he slept in the *sukkah*, he insisted on doing so. As his wife had foreseen, he caught a cold that turned into pneumonia.

As she plied him with tea and chicken soup, she remonstrated with him: "You see, *Chacham*, what happened to you because you slept in the *sukkah*." To which he replied, "You don't understand. It is true that I am sick because I fulfilled the *mitzvah* of dwelling in the *sukkah*. But can you imagine how sick I would have been if I hadn't fulfilled the *mitzvah* at all?"

In the eighteenth century, the Vilna Gaon said that the *sukkah* provided the Jew with a unique *mitzvah:* you can bring your entire self into the *sukkah*. It is unlike any other *mitzvah:* you enter it, eat in it, and if you are like that Hasid, you also sleep in it.

When we listen to the *shofar*, we use our ears. When we put on the *tfilin,* we use our arm and head. When we utter a *b'racha*, we use our voice.

But we enter the *sukkah* with our total being.

There are some very significant lessons in his comment.

First, he is suggesting that the most wonderful way to observe a *mitzvah* is with our total being. We came to the Synagogue on *Rosh Hashanah* and *Yom Kippur*. Now it is *Sukkot* and next week will be *Shmini Atzeret* and *Simchat Torah*. Then comes *Shabbat Breshit*. What a great habit to cultivate. It should be done every week.

Or take *shabbat*, for example. Coming to the Synagogue is one part of the observance. In our homes, we should light the candles, say the *Kiddush*, enjoy the *Shabbat* meal, and the family should spend time together. On *Shabbat* we should refrain from work, shopping, appointments, from all those activities which turn *Shabbat* into an ordinary day. To feel its full meaning, we have to observe *Shabbat* as a total, all-embracing experience.

Secondly, the *sukkah* into which we enter with our total being also teaches us the need for doing a *mitzvah* with total involvement. It is possible to do a *mitzvah* and to be thinking of something else. For example, fasting on *Yom Kippur*. The Prophet Isaiah in our *Haftorah* for *Yom Kippur* says:

> Is such the fast that I have chosen? . . .
> Is it to bow down his head as a bulrush
> And to spread sackcloth and ashes?

That is not what God wants, says the Prophet. He continues:

> Is not this the fast that I have chosen,
> To loose the fetters of wickedness . . .
> And to let the oppressed go free . . .
> Is it not to give your bread to the hungry,
> And to bring the poor who are cast out to your house?

You can fast, the Prophet says, and think of the wrong things; of how observant you are, of how hungry you are, of what you will eat at night, and you can forget the purpose of your fasting. The real meaning of fasting is to remind you of those people who are hungry, oppressed, and deprived throughout their lives and to pose the question to you: What are you willing to do about them?

Or take the *mitzvah* of prayer. It is possible to pray and to be a million miles away. Once, after he had finished *davening* the *Amidah*, Levi Yitzchak of Berdichev approached several people in his Synagogue, shook their hands, and greeted them several times with *Shalom Aleychem,* as though they had just come back from a long journey. When they looked at him in surprise, he said: "Why are you so surprised? You were far away, weren't you? You were in your store, you were on a ship with a cargo of grain, you were in the marketplace; and when the sound of *davening* ceased, then you returned. That is why I greeted you."

Total involvement in a *mitzvah* means to fast and to know why you are fasting; to pray with *kavanah*, with total concentration and feeling, attempting to exclude all distracting thoughts from your mind.

Furthermore, the *sukkah*, in the way it envelopes us, symbolizes the ideal pattern of Jewish living, which is that a Jew should surround himself with *mitzvot*.

In the recent CJP Community Survey of the Greater Boston Jewish Community, it was found that the observance of the Passover Seder and the gathering together with relatives for the Jewish holidays was high. But that is hardly enough for being a Jew. To be a Jew needs constant reminders, the constant doing of *mitzvot*.

It needs *sukkot* and *Simchat Torah*, and *meyah b'rachot*—reciting a hundred blessings each day. That is the reason that *kashrut* is so important—because it reminds us of our Jewishness three times a day.

The audacious attempt of Judaism is expressed in one great verse:

*V'hyitem li mamlechet kohanim v'goy kadosh:*
"You shall be unto Me a kingdom of priests and a holy nation."

The purpose of Judaism is to create for each of us a life of holiness, a constant awareness of the presence of God in our lives.

According to the Rabbis, there are two major categories of *mitzvot*:

*Mitzvot beyn adam lamakom:*
"The *mitzvot* between man and God," such as the rituals, and

*mitzvot beyn adam lachavero:*
"The *mitzvot* between man and his fellow man," such as the ethical commandments.

Some people choose one category but neglect the other. Some choose *beyn adam lamakom;* they are careful to observe every ritual but they are at the same time ethically bankrupt.

Last August in Jerusalem in the religious section of the city, the neighbors learned that one man in their midst, Shimshon Mizrachi, put on lights on *Shabbat*. One day, a group of young fanatics from the neighborhood broke into his home where he had lived all his life and destroyed every piece of furniture that he possessed. What a disgraceful example of *Chilul Hashem*, all in the name of religion!

There are other people who choose the *mitzvot beyn adam lachaveyro*. They are moved by great ethical concerns and they are involved in good causes, but Jewishly their lives are a virtual wasteland.

I remember how startled I was years ago to open a book by Walter Lippman, the great political commentator and columnist who was a Jew by birth, if not by conviction. The frontispiece to the book had these words: "Thou shalt love thy neighbor as thyself.—Matthew 19:19."

I suspect that Walter Lippman, great mind that he was, never realized that the original source of those sublime words is Leviticus 19:18 from our Torah.

The *sukkah* into which we enter with our entire selves symbolizes that the Jew must be concerned about God and man.

How does the beautiful biblical verse that we recite after every meal express this ideal? It says:

*V'nimtza cheyn v'seychel tov b'eyney elohim v'adam:*
"May we so live that we will find love and understanding in the eyes of God and man."

How, then, should a *mitzvah* be performed? If there is to be total involvement, each *mitzvah* should be done with special care and great beauty.

The Rabbis asked a question about the biblical verse which Israel sang after they crossed the Sea of Reeds:

*Zeh eyli v'anveyhoo:*
"This is my God and I will glorify Him."

They wondered: Is it then possible for a person of flesh and blood to add glory to his Creator? And they answered that the way in which we add to God's glory is by the manner in which we fulfill His *mitzvot*. They interpret the verse:

*Anaveh lo b'mitzvot:*
"I shall observe His Mitzvot with beauty.

*Eheseh l'fanav lulav naeh sukkah naah tzizit naah t'filin naah:*
"I shall prepare before Him a beautiful *lulav*, a beautiful *sukkah*, a beautiful *tallit*, beautiful *t'filin*."

## Living Courageously

If you are serious about doing a *mitzvah*, it must be given great thought and preparation if it is to be done with beauty. Therefore, the Rabbis developed the concept of *noy sukkah*, decorating the *sukkah* as beautifully as possible. The kind of beauty, for example, added to our Temple *sukkah* by our Sisterhood. The kind of beauty added to their *sukkot* by individuals in their use of tapestries, murals, bottles of wine and oil, symbols of the harvest, fruits, cranberries, and paper cutouts.

One of the Hasidic Rabbis, Rabbi Chaim of Tsanz, discouraged his Hasidim from going to great expense in decorating their *sukkot*. Instead, he asked them to follow his example by inviting poor people to eat with them in their *sukkot*. As he would explain: "Poor people are the most beautiful decorations of any *sukkah!*"

If a *mitzvah* demands total involvement, then there is only one dimension that is still missing. How shall a Jew perform a *mitzvah*? The Rabbis' answer was:

> *Eyn hashechinah shora elah mitoch simcha shel mitzvah:*
> "God's presence is only truly felt when we perform a *mitzvah* with rejoicing, with *simcha.*"

This is the joy of building a *sukkah* with the participation of the whole family. It is the joy of lighting the Menorah on Hanukkah, of reading the *Megillah* on Purim, of celebrating the Seder on *Pesach*. It is the joy of *Simchat Torah*, when we sing, dance, and cavort in total abandonment; in total love with Torah and with being a Jew.

As we enter our *sukkah* this year, bringing to it our entire selves, let us determine in the coming year to do the same with every *mitzvah* we fulfill.

# 16.
# Specialize in a *Mitzvah*

Rabbi Israel Salanter, who lived in Lithuania in the nineteenth century, was the founder of the Musar Movement, which placed its major emphasis on the ethical teachings of Judaism.

One of his teachings was that even though each Jew should try to fulfill all the *mitzvot*, in addition each person should adopt one *mitzvah* and make it his specialty, to perform it as often as possible, with great love and concern.

I was reminded of this teaching recently when I met a man who lives on Cape Cod who told me of the difficulty of being a Jew on the Cape; the problem of trying to get a *minyan* when you need one; the struggle to raise your children as Jews. But one of the *mitzvot* this man has taken upon himself for many years is to sell Israel Bonds, and he does a wonderful job. He searches out every Jew on the Cape and makes certain that each one buys an Israel Bond.

In the Hebrew weekly *Hadoar*, the writer Akiva ben Ezra tells about his uncle who was a *melamed* in a small town in Europe, whose name was Reb Hayim Itzik's. Reb Hayim took upon himself a special *mitzvah*. Every Friday afternoon, *Erev Shabbat*, he carried a large sack and went from house to house to collect rolls and bread for poor people. The women of the town would attempt to outdo each other in baking the best rolls possible so that they could give them to Reb Hayim Itzik's.

Ben Ezra also writes about another man, this one from Israel, who lives in Hadera, whose name is Yaakov Reznik. This man lost a son in Israel's War of Independence in 1948. Every *Erev Shabbat*, he loads up a number of boxes and places them on a military truck and brings them to a recreational area for Israeli soldiers. When he reaches the area, where he has built two special booths, he serves Israeli soldiers fruit, humus, tehina, bread, cake, and soda. Everybody in Hadera knows Yaakov Reznik. They call him *"meshuga l'chayalim*"—crazy about soldiers. What they do not know, adds the writer, is that often he uses the last dollar of his meager earnings to buy food for the soldiers. Yaakov Reznik has taken upon himself a special *mitzvah* in memory of his son.

Wouldn't it be wonderful if each of us would specialize in one particular *mitzvah*. There are so many to choose from, six hundred and thirteen in all. We could visit sick people, giving them words of encouragement. We could help the elderly so that they would not feel that they are abandoned and alone. We could help another person in trouble, who may be taking drugs, or may be having problems at home.

Why should we specialize in one particular *mitzvah*? Because to do a *mitzvah* well, we need to develop the expertise that comes only with experience. If we want to help those who are sick, we need to know what to say so that we are helpful rather than harmful.

Some people are afraid of older people. If we want to help them, we will need the experience to learn how to listen and how to encourage, how to become the answer to their prayer of "Al tashlicheynu l'eyt ziknah"—Cast us not off in our old age.

If we want to be of help to fellow Jews, in countries where they are being oppressed, we have to learn the most effective methods so that our efforts will really make a difference.

There is a second reason for specializing in a *mitzvah*. Most people perform a *mitzvah* as the mood strikes them. They do it once or twice, soon forget, and go back to their own preoccupations. But the specialist makes a *mitzvah* his special love. He fulfills it all his life regardless of his mood, regardless of the weather, regardless of inconvenience.

There is yet another reason for specializing in a certain *mitzvah*. It can transform us as human beings. To become a specialist in any field, whether in mathematics, music, or Talmud, demands hard work, self-discipline, practice every day, and great perserverance. That kind of discipline can carry over to the rest of our activities, to our habits of study and work. Furthermore, to specialize in a *Mitzvah* which helps people is to get to know people in the most profound way possible. We share their troubles, worries, and hopes. It gives us greater understanding and greater compassion, making us better people.

Finally, when you specialize in a *mitzvah*, it leaves you no time for complaints. Many people complain that they are tired, discouraged, unhappy. But when you wake up every day knowing you have to do your *mitzvah* in helping another person, there is no time left for the petty worries and complaints with which some people preoccupy themselves throughout their lives.

In conclusion, let me tell you about one more person who has taken upon herself a special *mitzvah*. Elie Wiesel has told this story of an elderly Jewish woman in New York who spends most of her time in the maternity ward of a hospital. She goes from room to room to ask if the prospective mother is Jewish. If she is, she asks permission to stay with her, to help her in every way possible, reassuring her and comforting her. She relieves the nurses of most of their responsibilities. This lady receives no salary and no task is too difficult for her.

Who is this lady? She is a survivor of Hitler's concentration camps where she lost all of her children. When she came to the United States after the war, she soon began to visit maternity wards in different hospitals. Each Jewish child that is born is her personal *simcha*, and when it is born, she always says these words:

*Dos yiddish folk hot bakumen noch a kind! mazal tov!*
"The Jewish people has acquired another child. *Mazal Tov!"*

This is her personal *mitzvah*, her personal affirmation, that despite everything the Nazis did to her and to our six million brethren, *am yisrael chai!*—the Jewish people will continue to live!

# 17.
# The Problem of Prayer

When we approach the prayer book, most of us feel that each of the prayers is an expression of the writer's profound faith. Just as when we approach the Bible, we think that every book in the Bible must be an expression of the most devout kind of faith.

And yet, when one studies the Bible carefully, one finds that there are certain books that are really very shocking. The Book of Job, for example, raises the most profound questions about a person's faith. Though it is true that there are expressions of faith in the book, we should also be aware that there were Rabbis in the talmudic period who thought that the Book of Job should not be in the Bible at all because of the many questions and challenges to faith it raises.

I would like to suggest to you that if you carefully examine the prayer *Ma Tovoo*, you will see in it an expression of faith, but it is the kind of faith that comes only after a prolonged and intense struggle.\*
*Ma Tovoo* is the prayer with which the Service begins and, as we usually read it, we likely see in it a prayer of great faith and affirmation. The question I would like to consider with you is why the Rabbis, who were very concerned about the order of prayer, chose this particular prayer to be placed at the beginning of the prayer book. I would like to study it with you to see whether we might find evidence of an internal struggle in the soul of the writer who is really very uncomfortable with prayer, just as I am certain that there are many of us who come into the Synagogue and have our own problems with prayer.

The prayer begins with the words that are very familiar to us: *"Ma tovoo ohalecha yaakov mishkenotecha yisrael,"*—How goodly are your tents, O Jacob, and your dwelling places, O Israel. This phrase is

---

\*I base the explication of this prayer upon an interpretation offered by Professor Reuven Kimmelman of Brandeis University.

taken from the Book of Numbers in the Bible, from a passage in which the soothsayer Balaam blesses the children of Israel. He observes the Israelites, temporarily settled from their wandering in the wilderness, and comments: "Everything looks so good as I observe your tents and your dwelling places, O Israel." The Talmud interprets these words, *"ohalecha,"* tents, and *"mishkenotecha,"* dwelling places, as referring to the Synagogues and the houses of study of the Jewish people. When Balaam saw the Israelites praying and studying, he foresaw the time when Jews would build Temples and houses of study in their future communities. It was a scene so memorable and beautiful to Balaam that he praised it in the most moving terms.

What happens today when a person enters a synagogue? He or she may be a person who may have struggled mightily with the problem of prayer. He looks about him as you, perhaps, have looked at our Temple this *Shabbat,* and says: *"Ma tovoo ohalecha yaakov"*—How beautiful are your synagogues, O Israel. But the next word after that verse is *"Va'ani"*—But I—a word that is repeated three times in this prayer. It is an unusual emphasis because the writer wanted us to see a special meaning here. It is true, he is saying that this is a beautiful Synagogue and that there are many people who are praying and who seem to know what they are doing, *"Va'ani,"* "but I" have great problems with this Synagogue and I am not at all sure that I know what I am doing here. The question is: Do I belong in this Synagogue with these prayers? Do I really belong here?

Some people have all kinds of problems with the Synagogue and with prayer. Some people have not studied Hebrew and, as a result, they find the language of the *Siddur* to be a problem. Some people are simply not accustomed to praying and they, therefore, don't know how to enter into the spirit of prayer. Some people have more profound questions, wondering if there is a God and whether He listens to prayer. Or, they question, is there any purpose to all of the prayers that people are reciting in this Synagogue? The person who composed this prayer also had these problems, expressed in the word *"Va'ani"*—"but I—I have problems with prayer."

Then he answers his own question: *"Va'ani b'rov chasdecha—"* But I know from what I have learned about you, dear God, that you have an abundance of goodness and love. Therefore, if You are indeed as good, loving, and accepting as people say You are, then I feel welcome in Your home."

Imagine coming to a party where everyone is enjoying himself and having a great time and suddenly you discover that you were not invited. What a terrible feeling! The people begin to sit down to dinner and there is no place for you. You are terribly embarrassed and you would love to be able to sink into the floor and disappear. But then the hostess hears about your plight, hurries over to you, and apologizes for your discomfort and says: "Please stay for dinner. We'd love to have you stay." You feel such a sense of relief—they do want me here after all, you think, I do belong. After that feeling of excruciating embarrassment, you now feel overwhelmingly grateful to the hostess for her graciousness. You sense that you are not really out of place and you decide to stay after all.

So, too, does God say to us when we are feeling uncomfortable: "I know that you feel awkward. I know that you have not been comfortable in this setting before, but please stay. Many good people have come in the same way, awkward and uncertain, but, eventually, after coming for a while, they have begun to feel comfortable and at home in My house."

Then the writer continues: "I feel very welcome, God, and I want to express my thanks to You, God." How does he express his gratefulness? In the Orient, when you want to express thanks, you bow down. Therefore, he says *"Eshtachaveh"*—"I will bow down in order to show my gratefulness and thanksgiving to You." To whom will he bow down? *"El heychal kodshecha"*—To Your Holy Ark. He does not yet bow down to God Himself but to that invisible symbol of God's presence, which is found in every Synagogue. I bow down, he says, to Your Ark, the symbol of Your presence.

And yet, he is not completely at home with God and, therefore, he says in the next words: *"B'Yiratecha"*—With a feeling of reverence for You, O Lord. It is not yet a feeling of intimacy or love which a person ought to feel toward God. So far, it's only a feeling of respect. It is similar to a person who has been welcomed to the home of a very important person whom he doesn't know well. He feels very respectful but he is still uncertain about what their relationship will be like.

Permit me to skip the next verse and let us look together at the penultimate verse. Again, it begins with *"Va'ani."* The writer is still struggling with theological questions but now he is beginning to feel more comfortable in the Synagogue. He is very grateful for this feeling and now he says: *"Eshtachaveh v'echraah evrecha"*—I will bow down. Before whom? *"Lifney Adonai Osi"*—I will bow down before God, my Creator. Now he is no longer bowing to the Ark, the symbolic presence of God, but he feels close enough to Him to be able to say, "I bow down before God Himself." He begins to feel closer to his host and more comfortable in His presence.

And then once again the same word, *"Va'ani."* "But I am still having problems about praying to God." I ask myself, "Though I do sense God's presence in this place, I would yet like to know whether He is available to me. God, the Creator of the Universe, who has so many concerns that are so vast, does He have any time or interest in little me? Do I have the right to bother Him and is this the right time to approach Him?" These are the questions going through the mind of the person who is struggling to try to pray to God. And he wants to know: "Is it *Eyt ratzon*—is it an opportune time to pour out my anguish and sorrow before God? Is it right to tell Him about my hopes and my dreams? And if I do, will He pay any attention to me?"

Once again, he answers himself with the same words that he used in the second verse, *"B'rov chasdecha"*: "Dear God, You have so much love. You are, after all, the source of all love, and You are always available to each person. You are always ready to respond to our needs and our feelings at each moment of our lives, whether we find ourselves in the depths of despair or in the heights of exultation."

Now, finally, this person feels himself sufficiently confident to begin to pray and this is where the first words of his prayer really begin. He says: *"Aneyni be'emet yishecha"*—Answer me, O Lord, with Your unfailing help.

He knows from his experience that people are not always dependable. Sometimes, our hearts may be filled with such despair but there is nobody to listen. Our spouse may be asleep. Our children may be busy. Our psychiatrist may be on vacation. But God is always available, always ready to listen and to help, and he gives us the strength and encouragement to endure whatever life brings our way.

This is the struggle that the writer experienced and the struggle that each of us must go through if we are ultimately to experience the meaning of prayer and God.

Now permit me to take you back to the first verse of this prayer for yet another moment. Why was this verse chosen to begin this prayer at the very beginning of the prayer book? It is a very special verse about which I didn't reveal the whole story before. I said that the reason the writer says it is because he knows that though some people feel good about the Synagogue, he himself had problems. But there is yet another reason why I believe the Rabbis chose this verse.

Do you remember the circumstances of Balaam's uttering these words? Balaak, the King of Moab, had called upon him, the expert soothsayer, to come to curse the Israelites. In ancient times people believed that certain people had the ability to curse or bless others and that their words would make a critical difference in the lives of these people. Balaam came willingly and was eager to curse Israel because Balaak had promised him a large remuneration for his curse. Balaam then observed the people, studied them from different vantage points, tried to curse them, but the only words which he could utter were: *"Ma tovoo ohalecha yaakov, mishkenotecha yisrael"*—How wonderful it is to observe this peaceful, law-abiding people. They don't want to go to war. You, King of Moab, are afraid of them needlessly. All they want to do is to pass through your land on their way to the Promised Land.

What makes these words so remarkable is that they were intended as a curse but they were transformed into a blessing. Perhaps you came to the Synagogue this morning with a feeling of great ennui or indifference, or perhaps you even came with a feeling of resentment, saying to yourself, "Why do I have to get stuck here this morning?" Perhaps you associated your coming to the Synagogue today with those memories of long ago when somebody used to force you to come to *Shul*, perhaps a parent or a grandparent.

But this prayer says to you: if you are willing to open your heart to the experience of prayer this *Shabbat*, if you are willing to open your heart to a community that is gathered not for the purpose of competition or for hurting one another, but to worship God and to feel closer to one another, then it is possible that unexpectedly you might find yourself uttering a prayer for help, or a prayer of hope, or a prayer of thanksgiving to God for all of the gifts and all of the blessings that He has given to you and to me and to all of us who are here this day.

The Hasidic Rabbi of Kotzk once entertained a group of learned visitors. These learned visitors were somewhat skeptical about the Rabbi because they were not Hasidim. He surprised them by asking them the question, "Where is the dwelling place of God?" They laughed at him, surprised that a learned Rabbi should ask such a question, and they responded, "Is not the whole earth full of His glory?" Then the Rabbi answered his own question by saying, "God dwells wherever a man lets Him in."

*Ma tovoo*—How good it will be if each of us will permit God to enter and transform our lives.

# 18.
# The Right Kind of Prayers

Psychologists tell us that whatever we do is a clue to our life-style: the way we walk and dress, our gestures and our manner of speaking. Everything we do is a clue to our inner personality.

The Rabbis of the Talmud add yet another dimension: they say that the way a person prays is also a clue to his philosophy of life. They therefore encourage certain kinds of prayers and discourage others. Some prayers, they feel, give greater meaning to life; others are harmful to the cultivation of a holy personality, which is our faith's ultimate goal.

What are the wrong kind of prayers? The Talmud says:

> *Hatzoek l'sheavar harey zo t'filat shav:*
> "To cry over the past is to utter a vain prayer."

The Mishnah cites this illustration of such a prayer. If your wife is pregnant, you should not pray, "May it be a boy!" because the gender of the child has already been determined.

*Hatzoek l'sheavar*: So many of us cry over the past. We say, "If only I had been a better mother or father, my child would have turned out so differently!" If a loved one dies, we cry, "If only I had been a better child, my parents would have been so much happier!" In our work we complain, "If only I had gone into another field, I would have really been happy . . ."

So many of us walk around burdened with guilt, constantly punishing ourselves, torturing ourselves with all the "if onlys" that did not happen. But the Talmud says:

> *Hatzoek l'sheavar harey zo t'filat shav:*
> "To cry over the past is to utter a vain prayer."

It is simply wasted energy and wasted emotions. The past is gone, it cannot be changed. The real question for each of us is: what are you doing with your life now, today? What are you doing about your relationships with the people around you, your family and friends? How are you doing in your work now? Are you trying to do it as well as you can? And are you deriving from it as much fulfillment as possible? Nobody's work is all bliss. Don't dwell only on the unpleasant aspects of your job. Try to think about the parts of your work that give you gratification as well.

When Victor Hugo was being persecuted by his beloved France, heartbroken, living in enforced exile, he would climb a cliff overlooking the harbor at sunset, select a pebble, and stand in deep meditation before throwing it into the water. He seemed to derive great satisfaction from performing this simple ritual each evening. Some children watched him throw the pebbles into the water, and one of them asked, "Why do you come here to throw these stones?" Hugo smiled and answered quietly, "Not stones, my child, I am throwing self-pity into the sea." To cry over the past is a vain prayer.

There is another kind of prayer the Rabbis discourage. If you are returning from a trip and you hear a cry of distress from your town and you pray:

*Yehee ratzon shelo yihyoo ayloo b'nai vayti*:
"God grant that this cry is not coming from my house!"

*harey zo t'filat shav*:
"This is a vain prayer."

First, because it has already been determined and your prayer cannot change the location. More important, it is an unethical prayer. You are hoping that the catastrophe has happened to somebody else! To pray at another's expense is to defeat the purpose of prayer.

Prayer is supposed to make us more sensitive to the needs of others. So many of our prayers are couched in the plural lest they become selfish prayers. We say:

*R'faeynu hashem v'neyrafey*:
"Heal *us*, O Lord, and *we* shall be healed."

*Barech aleynoo shanah tovah*:
"Bless *us* with a year of abundance."

> *Shma koleynu hashem elokeynu:*
> "Hear our voices, O Lord, our God, have compassion upon
> us . . ."

How should we pray in such a circumstance—upon hearing a cry of distress from the city? I suppose it should really be worded something like this:

> *Yehee ratzon shelo yikreh ason l'af echad, shekulam b'nai vayti:*
> "May it be Your will that no catastrophe befall any person,
> for every person is a part of my household."

The Hasidic Rabbi Mendel of Rymanov used to say that during the time he was reciting the *Amidah,* all the people who ever asked him to pray to God in their behalf would pass through his mind. Someone once asked him how that was possible, since there was surely not enough time. Rabbi Mendel replied: "The need of every person leaves a trace in my heart. In the hour of prayer, I open my heart and say: '*Ribono shel olam*: Lord of the Universe, read what is written here.' "

The purpose of prayer is to make us feel the needs of every person as well as our own.

What kind of prayers do the Rabbis encourage?

> *Chayav adam l'vareych al haraah keshem shehu mevareych al
> hatovah:*
> "It is incumbent upon a person to bless God in the face of
> evil as it is to bless Him for the good."

It is easy to believe in God when things go well, but the test of real faith is what happens when we are faced with disappointment, failure, and tragedy. The Talmud says that there is a profound difference between an idolater and a believer in God. To the idolater, if the idol grants him his wishes, he feeds him and worships him. If he does not fulfill his requests, he smashes the idol into a million pieces. But the true person of faith maintains his faith even when faced with the greatest catastrophe.

This is why we say *Kaddish* when we are bereaved, even though there is no mention of death in the prayer. It is a prayer of religious affirmation said at precisely the time when it is most difficult to do so. When we lose a loved one, we cry, "Why did this happen to me?"

And we want to reject God, religion, and faith. Yet our Tradition says: Rise together with the congregation and say:

*"Yitgadal v'yitkadash sh'mey rabbah":*
"Magnified and sanctified is His great name!"

In every life there are joys and sadness, lights and shadows. Someone once said, "We should not pray to God: 'God, please never let me suffer!' Everybody who lives, suffers, everybody has his share of *tzoros*. What we should pray is: 'Dear God, give me the strength to face whatever life brings my way.' "

Finally, the Rabbis encourage another kind of prayer:

*Banah bayit chadash v'kanah kaylim chadashim omeyr baruch shehecheyanu:*
If a person builds a new house, or buys new utensils, or new clothes, he should say *shehecheyanu*, he should give thanks to God.

Other authorities have added other occasions for saying *shehecheyanu*, for example, on the Holy Days, or in the performance of any *mitzvah* which is associated with happiness.

Our Tradition encourages us to give thanks for our many blessings. On *Rosh Hashanah* we should give thanks for our husband or wife, our parents, and our children. On Mother's Day we say a *shehecheyanu* for mothers, but why not every day of the year? Fathers are nice to have around, too, and we should give thanks for them every day as well. And though our children may cause us headaches and heartaches, life would really be very dull without them and would lose so much of its meaning, so we should thank God every day for our children.

So often we are unaware of our many blessings. The poet expresses this idea so well:

> Five thousand breathless dawns all new
> Five thousand flowers fresh in dew
> Five thousand sunsets wrapped in gold,
> One million snowflakes served ice-cold,
> Five quiet-friends; one baby's love;
> One white-mad sea with clouds above;
> One hundred music-haunted dreams

Of moon drenched roads and hurrying streams;
Of prophesying winds and trees;
Of silent stars and browsing bees;
One June night in a fragrant wood,
One heart that loved and understood,
I wondered when I waked at day
How—in God's name—I could pay.

What our Tradition really ecourages us to do is to say a *shehecheyanu* each day of our lives, to give thanks for each day and its untold possibilities for creativity, compassion, and love.

# 19.
# Private Prayer

Genuine prayer cannot be limited to the prayers that we say with the congregation. When the heart is full and the emotions are overflowing, each of us needs to say our own private prayers as well. Therefore, at each Service, our Tradition provides a time of Silent Devotion, a time when we should say our own prayers as well as those that are prescribed.

For example, the Rabbis say that when you say the prayer in the *Amidah*—

*Refaeynu hashem v'nayrafay:*
"Heal us, O Lord, and we shall be healed,"

if there is someone in your family or among your friends who is very ill, stop and add a private prayer for the person you love. Or, in the *Amidah*, when you say,

*Shema kolainu:*
"Hear our voice, O Lord our God"

if you have any special prayer you want to say, say it at that point, in your own words, expressing your own feelings.

In the Talmudic tractate *B'rachot*, which deals with the creation of our liturgy, there are recorded some of the private prayers of a number of Rabbis which they used to recite after they had concluded praying with the congregation. Some of those prayers were so beautiful and became so beloved that later Rabbis introduced them into the *Siddur*, the prayer book. We therefore have a number of private prayers that have become the prayers of the congregation.

For example, there is a very beautiful prayer that we recite on the *Shabbat* before *Rosh Chodesh*, a new Hebrew month. It begins with:

*Y'hi ratson:*
"May it be Your will, O Lord our God, that we have a life of health, strength, and of spiritual beauty."

This was originally a private prayer composed by Rav, who created it to express his own private emotions.

There is another prayer that so many of us love which we recite at the end of the *Amidah*. It begins with the words:

*Elokay n'tsor l'shoni meyrah:*
"O Lord, guard my tongue from evil and my lips from speaking guile."

This was the private prayer of Mar bar Rabbina, and once again, the Rabbis loved this prayer so much that they placed it at the end of the *Amidah* so that everyone might have the opportunity to say it.

I would like to tell you about several other private prayers which were composed by Rabbis that are not as familiar to us but have great meaning as well. The Talmud tells us that Rabbi Hiyya used to pray the following private prayer after he had finished praying with the congregation:

*Y'hi ratson milfanechah, adonay elohkeynu shet'hai Toratchah umanutainu:*
"May it be Your will, O Lord our God, that Your Torah may be our occupation."

"Occupation" in this context seems like a rather strange kind of word. When we think of occupation generally, we think of a means of earning a livelihood, a profession, a trade, or a business. But Rabbi Hiyya says that a Jew's occupation, or perhaps even better, his "preoccupation," should be the Torah. It is his way of saying that every Jew has to find time for the study of Torah throughout his life, whether he is going to high school, or college, or is already engaged in some kind of work. Our Tradition expects that as a Jew grows and matures, so, too, will his understanding of the Torah grow more profound and provide him with more fulfillment and greater meaning.

But there is another meaning to what Rabbi Hiyya was saying in his prayer. It is that whatever our work happens to be in life, the ethical teachings of the Torah must always serve as our guidelines and standards. And that holds true for every business, profession, and trade.

Even if a person happens to be a scientist, whose entire discipline is founded upon the quest for truth, unless ethical standards are uppermost, the scientific enterprise can become just as dishonest and corrupt as any other occupation.

There was a scandal that rocked the scientific community a while ago. It was described as a "Medical Watergate," and it happened at the Sloan-Kettering Cancer Institute in New York. Dr. William Summerlin, of that Institute, claimed that he was able to take skin from one individual and transplant it to another successfully even though the recipient had not received special drugs to suppress the usual immunological rejection of such transplants. In order to provide evidence for this heretofore impossible accomplishment, Dr. Summerlin painted black patches on white mice in order to make it appear that the animals had obtained skin grafts from black mice. He was not the only culprit in the deception. It appears that the blame has to be shared by the director of Sloan-Kettering, Dr. Robert Good. Dr. Good had been with Sloan-Kettering for just a short time and was very interested in attracting national attention and a great deal of money for the Institute. As a result, he placed tremendous pressure on all of his researchers to produce results as quickly as possible. He was, apparently, somewhat less concerned about the veracity of those results.

That is why Rabbi Hiyya said that each day a person ought to pray:

> *Y'hi ratzon milfanechah shet'hai Toratcha umanutainu:*
> "In whatever we do, O Lord, during the coming day, whatever our work happens to be, help us to make the ethical values of the Torah preeminent and help us to make them our preoccupation, our guide and our standard, so that whatever we might do shall also be in consonance with the teachings of Your Torah."

Rabbi Alexandrai used to say a different prayer after he had finished praying with the congregation. He said:

> *Y'hi ratzon milfanechah, adonay elohkeynu shetahmidainu b'keren orah v'al taamidainu b'keren chasheycha:*

"May it be Your will, O Lord our God, to place us in an illumined corner and not in a darkened corner."

And he continued:

*V'al yidveh libenu v'al yechshechu ainainu:*
"And let not our heart be sick nor our eyes darkened."

Each of us at times desperately needs the prayer of Rabbi Alexandrai. Each human heart at times becomes sick with despair. Each person's eyes are at times darkened with hopelessness. When we lose a person we love, when we are afflicted with illness and suffering, when we are disappointed by someone we love, when we feel that life has absolutely no meaning and there is no point in going on, when we have been placed by life in a *keren chasheycha*, in a darkened corner of the universe, that is when we need this prayer so very much.

*Shetahmidainu b'keren orah:*
"Dear God, illumine my corner of the universe regardless of the darkness that surrounds me."

John Milton was one of the greatest poets of all time, and his poem *Paradise Lost* is the monumental epic poem of the English language. Milton, however, did not write that poem. He could not because he was already blind at that stage of his life. Instead, he dictated this masterwork to his three daughters.

Milton gives us an insight into the soul of a blind man who is struggling for celestial light in his remarkable poem *Samson Agonistes*. It is a retelling of the biblical story of the blinded Samson striking out with his waning strength against his abysmal adversity. Milton was not only thinking of Samson when he wrote that poem. He was also saying that he himself, and every man, can triumph over tragedy and bring illumination to the darkest corner of the universe, if he refuses to be defeated by the tragedies that life often brings with it.

Finally, Rav Safra composed another prayer. He used to pray this prayer each day:

*Y'hi ratzon milfanecha adonay elohkeynu shetasim shalom*
 *b'famalyah shel maalah ub'famalyah shel matah:*
"May it be Your will, O Lord our God, to establish peace among the celestial family and among the earthly family."

Rabbi Safra pictures the angels above squabbling and fighting among themselves because each one is a patron of a particular nation. Each one is struggling for the ascendancy of his nation, and God has to make *shalom* between the heavenly family.

And if He has trouble with His angels, think of the troubles that He has with us here on earth—with so many nations always battling, so many young people always dying, and so many families always being bereaved.

We need Rabbi Safra's prayer so much in our world "that God will somehow help us to create *shalom* here on earth as well as in heaven." We need desperately a time like that envisioned by the prophet Isaiah, when men shall learn war no more. We need a time like that envisioned by the little girl in a poem by Carl Sandburg.

The little girl saw her first troop parade and asked, "What are those?"

"Soldiers."

"What are soldiers?"

"They are for war. They fight, and each tries to kill as many of the other side as he can."

The girl was quiet for a moment. "Do you know, I know something."

"Yes, what is it you know?"

"Sometime they will give a war and nobody will come!"

*Y'hi ratzon milfanecha, shetasim shalom b'famalyah shel maalah ub'famalyah shel matah:*
"May it be Your will to establish peace among the celestial family and among the earthly family."